WHERE IS YOUR ETERNAL DESTINY
HEAVEN OR HELL

VI LINDEMUTH

Tremendous Leadership
PO Box 267 • Boiling Springs, PA 17007
(717) 701 - 8159 • (800) 233 - 2665 • www.TremendousLeadership.com

Where is Your Eternal Destiny: Heaven or Hell. Copyright © 2022 by Vi Lindemuth. All rights reserved. Unless otherwise indicated, all Scripture references are taken from the New Living Translation. Copyright © 1996, 2004, 2007, 2013, 2015 by Tyndale House Publishers, Inc. Used by permission. All rights reserved. No part of this book may be reproduced or transmitted in any form or by any means, electronic or mechanical, including photocopying, recording, or by any information storage and retrieval system, without permission in writing from the publisher, except by a reviewer, who may quote brief passages in review.

Tremendous Leadership's titles may be bulk purchased for business or promotional use or for special sales. Please contact Tremendous Leadership for more information.

Tremendous Leadership and its logo are trademarks of Tremendous Leadership. All rights reserved.

ISBN-13 978-1-949033-83-0 (book)
ISBN-13 978-1-949033-84-7 (ebook)

DESIGNED & PRINTED IN THE UNITED STATES OF AMERICA

DEDICATION

I dedicate this book to my Lord and Savior, Jesus Christ. Without His help and guidance, there would be no book. Also, He gave me a deep desire to tell people the truth regarding the afterlife.

DEDICATION

TABLE OF CONTENTS

Appreciation vii
Prologue ix

Introduction: Heaven and Hell 1
1   The Wages of Sin 3
2   Jesus Paid the Price 5
3   Lazarus and the Rich Man 8
4   Daniel in The Lions' Den 10
5   The Fiery Furnace 12
6   Noah and the Ark 14
7   Sodom and Gomorrah 16
8   Decisions 17
9   Belief 20
10   Mixed Bag 23
11   No Do-overs 25
12   Protection 26
13   Punishments 27
14   Obedience 30
15   No Escape 31
16   Maggots and Worms 33
17   Paradise 35
18   Reunions or Isolation 37
19   No Communication 40
20   No Water 42
21   Separation from God 44

22	Desperation	47
23	Optimist vs. Pessimist	48
24	Rehab and Hell	50
25	Dependency	53
26	Total Darkness	54
27	Music	56
28	Laughter	58
29	The Best Home	60
30	Quality or No Quality	63
31	Two baskets	65
32	Enemies	75
33	Judgment	78
34	Two Locked Doors	80
35	Good and Bad People	82
36	Different Roads	84
37	Satan Lies	88
38	Lake of Fire	90
39	New Jerusalem	93
40	Predicted Future Event	96
41	Future Return	98
42	Celebrated or Mourned	103
43	The Bible	107
44	Life, Death, and the Afterlife	108
45	Verses Found in the Bible	113

Epilogue 211

About The Author 215

APPRECIATION

I am appreciative and thankful for these people. Each of them guided and helped me during the entire book process.

My publisher, Tracey, was always professional, patient, and kind to me when I kept making change after change after change. I can never thank her enough.

The insight, knowledge, and skill of my proofreader, Heather, were invaluable.

Tim is a highly talented artist. All of his book covers were hard to pick from because all of them were phenomenal.

PROLOGUE

Do you believe in life after death? Do you accept that there is an afterlife? Do you know there are only two locations in the afterlife? Do you believe that the Bible clearly teaches about Heaven and Hell? Finally, do you know, beyond a shadow of a doubt, that you can choose where you want to live permanently in the afterlife?

The correct answers to my questions are noted below.

1. There is life after death on the earth.
2. There is an afterlife.
3. The only two locations in the afterlife are Heaven and Hell.
4. The Bible clearly teaches about Heaven and Hell.
5. Everyone will have to choose where they want to reside in the afterlife.

Death happens when you least expect it. Everyone is born, and everybody will die. When everybody dies, they will instantly enter the afterlife. God <u>is</u> very forthright with the truth. He does <u>not</u> use the surprise tactic. God does <u>not</u> want anyone blindsided. He makes it perfectly clear in the Bible what to expect in the afterlife. Everyone has to come to grips that the afterlife is going to happen; it is non-stoppable and non-avoidable.

Immediately entering the afterlife, everybody who <u>opts</u> for Heaven will be exuberant, ecstatic, and euphoric. They will <u>always</u> be smiling because of their happiness. On the other hand, the people who <u>did not</u> decide on Heaven will be paralyzed with fear, horror-struck, and panic-stricken in Hell. These people will <u>always</u> be frowning because of their unhappiness.

Where is Your Eternal Destiny

The reason that I wrote this book is to make the absolute truth known. Everyone will be permanent residents in Heaven (future New Jerusalem City) or Hell (future Lake of Fire) for trillions and trillions and trillions of years with no ending in sight.

The bottom line regarding the permanent afterlife residency is that it is a personal choice.

INTRODUCTION
HEAVEN AND HELL

I heard about a pastor presiding over a funeral. There was a large crowd that had come to pay their respects. As he spoke to them, the pastor explained that just as we all live, we all will die and, on the other side of death, will either be heaven or hell. He said that the Bible tells us we are all sinners, who have fallen short of the glory of God, and that the wage of sin is death (Romans 6:23). Because we as sinners can never repay our debt, God sent His only Son to die on the cross and pay for our sins.

The gift of salvation is free. Everybody has to make a personal choice to either accept or reject the gift. For those who accept Jesus as their Lord and Savior and turn from their sin, God cleanses them of all wickedness (1st John 1:9). Acceptance of salvation assures the people that they will spend eternity with God in heaven. On the other hand, those who reject salvation will find themselves eternally separated from Him in hell.

The pastor explained to the funeral attendees that this is the most critical decision you can make in your lifetime and will significantly impact your life more than who you marry, where you live, or what job you take. The pastor emphasized that they should not procrastinate in deciding to either accept or reject Jesus. He reminded them that God makes many promises in the Bible, but He never promises us another day.

After the pastor finished speaking, he left the podium, walked to the back of the room, and sat in a comfortable chair.

As he was sitting in the chair, he slumped over and died without any warning. His death happened mere minutes after he left the podium. Just as he warned the funeral crowd, he had no way of knowing how soon his final moment would come.

CHAPTER 1
THE WAGES OF SIN

After I put gasoline into my car one morning, I drove a short distance and got into the left-turn lane. Unfortunately, the traffic light got stuck and skipped the left-turn lane signal not once but seven times. Yes, I was counting and becoming angrier with each passing minute. Even though the traffic was heavy, I ultimately switched lanes and drove to the next traffic signal.

I became so mad at myself because I allowed my emotions to control me instead of me controlling my emotions. My behavior was sinful, and I had no excuse for my actions. God reminded me I needed to acknowledge my anger, confess my sin, and ask for His forgiveness. I didn't need to beat myself up; instead, I should make every effort not to repeat what I had just done in the future.

What does everyone have in common with me? Everybody is a sinner. We all sin every day, knowingly and unknowingly. Sometimes we think our sins are not a big deal, such as being irritated over a traffic light. Then, we blame our behavior and reactions on our circumstances for making us sin, such as claiming we were just tired, hungry, overwhelmed, or driven to irritation. We are all a total mess when it comes to sinning.

We can either choose to take responsibility or make up lame excuses. When people take responsibility, they become accountable for the charges against them. Most of us hate taking responsibility for the wrong things we do, think, and speak. We often use excuses to justify our sinful nature. We all have overblown egos, out-of-control emotions, pride, stupidity, stubbornness, and a lack of shame regarding our sins.

There are two ways we can respond when confronted with our own sin. One is hard to do, and the other is easy. Of course, taking full responsibility for our sins is hard. But, on the other hand, making excuses to ease the guilt of our sin is very easy.

A wage is earned. I thought about people earning wages and then paying a monthly bill with the money they earned. However, the Bible says the wages of sin is death (Romans 6:23). That is one debt that can never be paid off in monthly installments. Therefore, no amount of money can pay off the debt of our sins.

Jesus willfully died a horrific death to pay for every sin that we have done in the past, are committing right now, and will do in the future. He paid for every sin for all of humanity by His death on the cross.

CHAPTER 2
JESUS PAID THE PRICE

When Jesus was living on Earth, He taught numerous crowds of people about hell. Jesus was very serious regarding this subject. In Mark 9:43, Jesus said, "If your hand causes you to sin, cut it off. It's better to enter eternal life with only one hand than to go into the unquenchable fires of hell with two hands." He taught that hell does exist. It is a place of never-ending torments. No early releases are ever granted.

Jesus lived on the Earth for 33 years, and He led a perfect life. He was sinless and blameless the entire time. In 2nd Corinthians 5:21, we read, "For God made Christ, who never sinned, to be the offering for our sin, so that we could be made right with God through Christ." Despite His faultless life, Jesus was falsely accused and subjected to unfair and illegal trials. He endured emotional, mental, and physical abuse, tolerated humiliation and rejection, and withstood unimaginable anguish. Even though Jesus never sinned, He died an excruciating and horrifying death on the cross for us!

Most of us today cannot even imagine what Jesus endured before and during His death on the cross. Before Jesus was hung upon the cross, He was brutally beaten, blindfolded, and His beard was plucked out. Jesus was repeatedly struck in the face with the soldiers' fists, mocked, and spit on. After they placed a crown of thorns upon His head, the soldiers hit the sharp thorns with their staffs to drive them deeper into His head. The soldiers avoided touching the thorns themselves because they were so painful.

Jesus was ruthlessly scourged. Being scourged was a severe punishment that involved flogging with a lead-tipped whip.

Before a soldier would whip a person, they took off his clothes. The soldiers beat Jesus from His shoulders to His loins so violently that His skin was torn open, and His bowels were exposed.

As a result, Jesus' appearance was unrecognizable. He was bleeding, covered in deep bruises, and His skin was hanging off His body. Jesus' suffering was excruciating and unspeakable. After the whipping, the soldiers made Jesus walk more than three city blocks. Simon of Cyrene was told he had to carry the crossbar that weighed between 80 to 110 pounds because Jesus was too weak to hold it Himself.

Upon Jesus' arrival at Golgotha, the soldiers nailed Jesus to the cross. Heavy metal spikes seven to nine inches long were driven through His wrists and ankles, and He had to push up with His feet to even draw breath. Jesus was on the cross for six excruciating hours. He paid the maximum price for all of humanity when He died on the cross. His death bore our sin debts in full.

Jesus' death on the cross shows that God is loving and just. God loves us and longs for a relationship, but sin separates us from Him. The payment for that sin is death. God, in His love for us, sent His only son to Earth to live as a man and ultimately pay the price for our sin with His death. Through Jesus, God has given us freedom from our sin and a connection with Him. However, because God also demands justice for wrongs, those who do not accept Jesus and turn from sin will spend eternity separated from God.

Everyone loves to receive a gift, no matter their age. When you <u>accept</u> the free gift of salvation, you will spend eternity with God in heaven. You are permanently released from your sins.

People who <u>reject</u> the free gift of salvation will go to hell. They will be held accountable for their past and present sins and forced to endure all of the eternal punishments that are too awful for words. Jesus paid the highest price ever, giving us the freedom to choose either heaven or hell as our eternal destiny. We have the free will to decide where we will spend eternity.

CHAPTER 3

LAZARUS AND THE RICH MAN

The Bible tells us about someone who went to hell and what they experienced there. In Luke 16:19-31, Jesus speaks of a rich man who was very powerful, well-known, and respected in his community. He wore expensive clothes, ate the finest foods, and drank the best wine. However, the rich man was mean-spirited. He had no compassion or tolerance for people he thought were beneath him, and he refused to help others.

The rich man viewed life as all about him because he was self-absorbed. He was only concerned about his well-being. He believed himself to be extremely important and influential and concentrated solely on how he could sustain his opulent lifestyle.

A poor beggar was at the entrance gate of the rich man's residence. His name was Lazarus. He was disabled, hungry, poor, sick, and totally dependent on other people to meet his daily needs.

Every time the rich man saw Lazarus, he blew him off as though he never existed. The rich man thought Lazarus was an irritant and a pain in the neck. He wanted Lazarus to leave the gate entrance leading to his home immediately.

The rich man and Lazarus both died on the same day. The rich man closed his eyes on the Earth and instantly found himself in hell. Lazarus closed his eyes on the Earth but did not find himself in hell.

The rich man in hell is alive, conscious, and aware of his surroundings. He can communicate, reason, and think. However, he is isolated from other people, incredibly thirsty,

Lazarus and the Rich Man

and extremely hot. He is very uncomfortable and unable to escape.

The rich man is denied all types of freedoms. He experiences no contentment. The rich man is not given any of the luxuries he indulged in on Earth. The rich man is in terrible anguish because of the numerous kinds of torment. He is forced to face the reality of his new life.

The rich man remembers his past life on Earth and is extremely concerned about his five brothers, who are still alive. He wants someone to warn his brothers to repent so they can avoid hell.

Jesus taught many things using parables, but the rich man and Lazarus are factual and not a parable story. The rich man does exist. He has been in hell for over 2,000 years and is still there today.

CHAPTER 4

DANIEL IN THE LIONS' DEN

The Bible shows us countless examples of men who sought after God and were the recipients of His favor. Those who ignored Him did not receive favor; instead, they received His punishment. The lives of these men remind us that God is loving but also holy and just. One such example is found in the book of Daniel in the Old Testament.

Daniel was one of three administrators who supervised the high officers and protected the king's interests. Daniel was highly talented and outshined his two work associates. However, it did not take long for the other two men to become jealous and threatened by Daniel's success.

King Darius noticed Daniel's abilities and made plans to promote him to supervise the entire empire. Upon hearing about Daniel's future promotion, the two men and other government officials started to look for any mishandling of matters by Daniel, but they could find nothing. Daniel was a man of integrity.

The men secretly conspired against Daniel. They went to King Darius and urged him to enact a new law. People would be severely punished or killed when found worshipping God or anyone other than the King. He took their advice and enacted the new and irrevocable law for thirty days.

Despite the new law's enactment, Daniel still chose to pray three times a day to God and worship Him. The men showed up at Daniel's home unannounced and found him praying to God. They told King Darius about Daniel and what they saw him doing. Because King Darius favored Daniel, he tried to find a way around the new law but was unsuccessful. Finally, he had no choice but to order Daniel thrown into the lions' den.

As Daniel was lowered, a stone was placed over the opening, so there was no escape. The lions in the den were enormous, powerful, and hungry. They looked at Daniel as their next meal. Daniel prayed instead of worrying about the lions attacking him, and God heard and answered his prayers. God did a miracle right before Daniel's eyes. God sent an angel to shut the lions' mouths so they could not attack. He kept Daniel perfectly safe from the lions. Daniel spent the whole evening in the lions' den. After the mouths of the lions were shut, he was very much at ease. Daniel did not lose sleep because he knew God was protecting him.

Unlike Daniel, King Darius did not spend the night in peace. He was so disturbed at the thought of Daniel's death that, early the following day, he ran to the lions' den and yelled for him. King Darius was so relieved when he heard Daniel tell him he was okay because God shut the mouths of the lions.

King Darius was so frustrated with his advisors that he ordered every one of them, along with their wives and children, to be thrown into the lions' den. Before they reached the den's floor, the lions leaped up in the air and viciously tore them apart. King Darius' advisors and their families <u>did not belong</u> to God. God did not protect them; unfortunately, they died a terrifying death.

How did the same lions treat Daniel? Daniel was not attacked. He did not have one scratch on his body. Every lion instantly obeyed God and did not harm Daniel in any way. Daniel <u>belonged</u> to God.

There is a bottom line. Deciding to <u>belong to God</u> is the wisest decision. Choosing <u>not to belong to God</u> is incredibly tragic and leads to catastrophic consequences. What is your personal choice regarding this matter?

CHAPTER 5

THE FIERY FURNACE

The book of Daniel in the Old Testament gives us another example of God's love for those who follow Him. In Daniel 3:1-30, we learn that there was a king, and his name was Nebuchadnezzar. He made a gold statue ninety feet tall and nine feet wide. The figure was set up on the plain of Dura in the province of Babylon.

King Nebuchadnezzar enacted a new decree. The herald loudly proclaimed that the nations and people of every language were to fall down and worship the gold statue. Anyone refusing to fall down and worship the statue when they heard the sound would immediately be thrown into a blazing furnace.

The advisors told King Nebuchadnezzar about three young people. Their names were Shadrach, Meshach, and Abednego. All three young men flat-out refused to have anything to do with the king's statue. They ignored the king's command and refused to worship the gold statue. Shadrach, Meshach, and Abednego were brought before King Nebuchadnezzar. The king was furious and flew into a rage. King Nebuchadnezzar gave them one more chance to change their minds, but they declined.

The king immediately ordered some of the strongest soldiers in his army to securely tie up Shadrach, Meshach, and Abednego and throw them into the blazing furnace. In addition, he ordered the furnace to be heated seven times hotter than usual. Because it was so hot, the flames killed all of the soldiers while they were throwing the three young men into the scorching furnace. When Shadrach, Meshach, and Abednego were thrown into the blazing furnace, they were wearing robes, trousers, turbans, and other clothes. These things could have easily caught on fire.

King Nebuchadnezzar looked inside the fiery furnace and could not believe his eyes. He saw all three of the young men, together with another person, walking around untied in the fire unharmed. The king commanded Shadrach, Meshach, and Abednego to step out of the blazing furnace.

God spared the lives of Shadrach, Meshach, and Abednego. When they stepped out of the fiery furnace, their bodies were unharmed. Their hair was not singed, their clothes were not burned, and they did not smell like smoke. They did not suffer at all.

When King Nebuchadnezzar saw this, he enacted a new decree commanding everyone to stop worshipping the gold statue. All the people were instantly ordered to only worship God and no other gods. If anyone refused to do so, they would die a brutal death.

God was with Shadrach, Meshach, and Abednego. They were not afraid of their dreadful predicament but were very much at ease because they trusted God exclusively. Shadrach, Meshach, and Abednego knew God was with them and would protect them from the life-threatening and blazing heat inside the fiery furnace.

God does exist. For those who acknowledge Him with their lives, He will acknowledge them in the afterlife. But those who turn their back on Him on Earth will find He has turned His back on them in the afterlife. Separation from God is a dreadful and eternal consequence.

CHAPTER 6

NOAH AND THE ARK

Another example of God's love for man and justice towards the disobedient is found in the life of Noah. In Genesis 6-9, we read the people wanted nothing to do with God. They rejected, turned their backs, and deliberately ignored Him. The people were cruel, evil, vicious, and enjoyed living their life in wrong ways.

Noah was the opposite. He never ignored God. Instead, Noah strived to live his life in a way pleasing to God, being gentle, non-violent, and peaceful. As a result, Noah found great favor with God.

God instructed Noah to build an ark. He told Noah to build the ark 450 feet long, 75 feet wide, and 45 feet high. The structure had a roof; below the top was an opening one-cubit high all around. Noah constructed a door on the side of the ark. Inside there were lower, middle, and upper decks. It took Noah 120 years to finish the project assigned to him.

While building the ark, Noah told the people to repent and turn away from their lifestyles because of God's disapproval. The people laughed and ridiculed him. Noah told them there would be a great flood, but they did not believe him.

Once the ark was completed, God told him to get into it with his wife, sons—Shem, Ham, and Japheth—and their wives. Then God caused the 25,000 different kinds of animals to come to the ark on their own. When the last animal entered the ark, <u>God closed the door</u>. It is important to notice that <u>Noah did not close the door</u> (Genesis 7:16).

Shortly after the ark door was closed, it started to rain. It was not a soft and gentle rain; instead, it was a deluge. A deluge is a great downpour of rain where massive land areas become flooded. The surge caused the people to become frantic, high-strung, panicked, and even terrified.

The water began to rise higher and higher. I envision the people doing their very best to get Noah's attention by yelling at the top of their lungs, surrounding the entire ark, and pounding on the ark with their fists. They must have desperately wanted him to open the door so that they would survive. The panicked people fled to higher ground to escape but to no avail. They all drowned because of their failed attempts to get Noah to open the ark door.

Time ran out. It was too late for the people to change their minds. They were not given another chance to repent. All of the people died. There were no survivors.

God was in complete control of the ark door. He closed it and never reopened it for the people outside the ark. Remember, no human being can close what God opens, and nobody can open what God shuts.

CHAPTER 7

SODOM AND GOMORRAH

Another story that shows how much God hates sin is the story of Sodom and Gomorrah in Genesis 18-19. The people indulged in all different types of grievous sins they found enjoyable. God was infuriated at their disobedience. He decided to destroy Sodom and Gomorrah, as well as three neighboring towns named Admah, Zeboyim, and Lasha.

There was a righteous man, and his name was Lot. God allowed Lot and his family to safely escape Sodom and Gomorrah because they strived to please Him. After Lot and his family left, God destroyed Sodom and Gomorrah and the neighboring towns. God rained down burning sulfur, killing all of the people and vegetation. Nothing survived God's attack. Sodom and Gomorrah and the three surrounding towns were burned to ashes. The smoke rising was like smoke from a furnace.

With both Noah and Lot, we see the extent of God's wrath towards disobedience. We see how seriously He treats sin for those who reject His warnings and turn their back on Him. Yet, we also see how He spared Noah and Lot, just as He promised. "But the Lord will redeem those who serve Him. No one who takes refuge in Him will be condemned" (Psalm 34:22).

CHAPTER 8

DECISIONS

We live in a broken, fallen, and imperfect world. Because of that, we may endure hardships like the death of loved ones, disease, and divorce. Life on Earth has ups and downs, good times and challenging times, successes and failures, blessings and unexpected curve balls that knock us off our feet. But regardless of how our individual story unfolds, we all have these four things in common:

1. Everyone is born.
2. Everybody will live their life on Earth.
3. Everyone will die.
4. Nobody will ever be seen again on the Earth after they die.

Many people admit they are scared of dying, so they refuse to think about it. They do not want to attend the funerals of their families, friends, acquaintances, or coworkers. When they go to funerals, they want it to be over quickly. Funerals are a grim reminder to us that one day our lives on Earth will end. If someone is uncertain where they will spend eternity, the thought of death may make them uneasy or even frightened.

Another group anticipates and looks forward to entering the afterlife because they know they will spend it with their Heavenly Father, who loves them and sent His only son to die for them.

How would you answer these questions?

1. Which group are you in?
2. Does the thought of dying scare you because you are uncertain of what you will experience in the afterlife?

3. Do you have inner calmness and peace when thinking about your death?
4. Where are you going to spend eternity?

* * * * *

Most of us decide where we want to live and if we wish to rent or purchase. Before making our decision, we will consider different factors. For example, we might look at our financial budget, surrounding neighborhoods, safety, school districts, nearby eating and retail establishments, travel proximity to work, the availability of public transit and the associated costs. Most of us put so much effort into this decision because we want to make the very best choice, knowing that where we call home can significantly impact our day-to-day happiness.

HELL: People did not want to come here; instead, they wanted to go to heaven. Here are some reasons that people ended up in hell:

1. They were dependent on themselves rather than God. They believed that their works—being a good person, embracing high moral standards, helping other people and their community, making financial contributions to worthy causes, and volunteering their time – would earn them a place in heaven.
2. They refused to change their sinful lifestyle, even though they knew of God's disapproval.
3. Did not ask God's forgiveness of their sins.
4. Followers of false spiritual leaders who were affiliated with religious cults that did not preach God's truth.
5. No interest in spiritual matters whatsoever.
6. Refused to believe that Jesus is the only way to heaven.

Everybody made poor choices. They refused to take personal accountability for their wrong decisions. Angry at God for sending them to hell, the people are full of rage. God gives everyone the free will to choose how they want to live and where they will spend eternity.

HEAVEN: Everybody made the right decision. They decided to accept the truth that Jesus is the only way to heaven and nothing else. Everybody personally accepted Jesus.

* * * * *

Will you opt to make the <u>wrong</u> decision and end up in hell?
Will you opt to make the <u>right</u> decision and end up in heaven?

CHAPTER 9

BELIEF

When we cannot see, touch, or even taste something, we may question whether or not it exists. When something exists, it is real. When something is not real, it does not exist.

God does exist. He is very much alive at this very moment. God will never cease to exist, disappear, or die in the future. He will be around forever. The Bible says, in Revelation 22:13, "I am the Alpha and the Omega, the First and the Last, the Beginning and the End."

The afterlife does exist. No one can sidestep it. All of humanity will instantly enter the afterlife once they die on Earth because it is inescapable. The Bible gives us the facts regarding the afterlife. It teaches us what to expect. God inspired the Bible from Genesis to Revelation. The Bible is infallible. We can trust it implicitly. The Bible is 100% guaranteed to be the absolute truth and nothing but the truth.

From the Scriptures, we also know that Satan exists. 1st John 3:8 tells us, "But when people keep on sinning, it shows that they belong to the devil, who has been sinning since the beginning. But the Son of God came to destroy the works of the devil." Satan has dreadful character traits. He is the ultimate bully, con-artist, deceiver, slanderer, schemer, and stalker. His mission is to deceive and mislead as many people as he can. Satan does this to get even with God because of his utter hatred towards God and the entire human race.

God's adversary is Satan. In Revelation 12:7-9, we learn that Satan was once an angel who rebelled against God and was cast out of heaven. God knows where he is at all of the

Belief

time. Satan <u>has never</u> controlled Him. In the book of Job, we see that Satan had to get God's permission before he could bring calamity upon Job, a true follower of God (Job 1:12).

From the Bible, we also know that demons exist. In Ephesians 6:12, we read, "For we are not fighting against flesh and blood enemies, but against evil rulers and authorities of the unseen world, against mighty powers in this dark world, and against evil spirits in the heavenly places." God knows the names of every demon and where they are every second of the day and night. Demons are powerfully built, but character-wise they are cowardly and fearful. The demons loathe all of humanity. Their mission is to cause the entire human race acute emotional, mental, and physical distress regardless of age, gender, nationality, or religious beliefs.

Every demon knows who God is, as well as what is going to happen to them in the future. Knowing the upcoming outcome is making them scared stiff. The demons know that God will significantly punish them to the highest degree. Their afflictions are going to be off-the-charts. Every demon physically trembles at the thought of God.

Because of His deep love for man, God wants humanity to know about the afterlife before they arrive at their final eternal destination. He does not want anybody to be surprised and unprepared. Some people plan and prepare for the afterlife before they arrive. Other people refuse to even think about where they will spend eternity. Are you prepared or unprepared for the afterlife?

* * * * *

Will you opt <u>not</u> to believe that the afterlife and God exist?
Will you opt to <u>believe</u> that the afterlife and God exist?

* * * * *

Where is Your Eternal Destiny

When people purchase a brand-new vehicle, they receive an owner's manual. It tells them about their car and what to do when things start going wrong. The Bible is like an owner's manual. It tells people what will happen to them after they die and enter the afterlife. Likewise, the Bible warns of what <u>will</u> happen in the future. The owner's vehicle manual informs the owner of what <u>could</u> happen in the future.

* * * * *

Will you opt <u>not</u> to believe the Bible regarding the afterlife and what to expect?

Will you opt to <u>believe</u> the Bible regarding the afterlife and what to expect?

CHAPTER 10
MIXED BAG

Life is like a very colorful mixed bag containing all types of experiences. There are good and bad times, happiness and disappointments, victories and setbacks, and successes and failures. The mixed bag includes both positive and negative things. It is truly a mixed bag.

Recently, somebody asked me a question. They wanted to know if their <u>present</u> life on Earth would be better than their <u>future</u> life in the afterlife. The afterlife offers two types of life. It is either going to be astounding or atrocious. Everybody will be forced to make their personal decision regarding their eternal life. They have to decide what kind of life they want to experience in the afterlife that will be ongoing forever and ever. The best or worst is yet to come. There are no mixed bags found in eternity. It is either all good or all bad.

There are only two afterlife locations. One location is the greatest, with incredible and positive things always happening. The other location is the worst, with appalling and negative things that are never-ending. Most people want to reside in the very best location.

<u>**HELL**</u>: There are no mixed bags here. The only bag is massive, heavy, and ugly. Inside the bag, there are only bad things found. These things are affecting everyone emotionally, mentally, and physically. It is a lose-lose situation.

The absolute worst place is hell. It <u>should be</u> avoided at all costs. The quality of life it offers is very tragic. Everyone wants to escape the atrocious agonies, pains, punishments, and sufferings, caused by God's righteous judgment and wrath.

Unfortunately, nobody is given an enjoyable and optimal life in hell. Instead, it is dangerous, dreadful, eerie, ferocious, horrific, and horrendous.

<u>HEAVEN</u>: Heaven is a fantastic place. It is truly the most excellent, the finest, and the greatest. There are only wonderful, mind-boggling, and unbelievable things found here. It is genuinely a win-win situation. It offers a quality of life that is out-of-this-world.

Everybody is very much alive. Nobody here wants to leave because nothing bad, evil, distressing, harmful, wicked, or upsetting ever happens. On the contrary, only magnificent and unimaginable things occur here daily.

* * * * *

Will you opt <u>to reside</u> in hell, which is the worst place?
Will you opt <u>to reside</u> in heaven, which is an amazing place?

CHAPTER 11
NO DO-OVERS

Have you ever heard the term "mulligan?" It's a golf term that means "do-over." If a golfer's first shot doesn't go as planned, they can take a mulligan, meaning try again. What a fantastic idea that if we make a mistake, we can get a do-over!

<u>HELL</u>: Unfortunately, there are no do-overs here. People are eternally separated from God with no second chances to choose Him. Some people refuse to believe in hell because they think a loving God would never send anyone there. Just as we have seen in the lives of Noah, Daniel, and Lot, God is a loving God, but He also demands righteousness. Once people arrive in hell, it is too late to make the right choice.

<u>HEAVEN</u>: The do-over approach is unnecessary!

* * * * *

Will you opt to be <u>denied</u> the opportunity for a do-over in hell? Will you opt to <u>never need</u> a do-over in heaven?

CHAPTER 12
PROTECTION

Most of us want to be protected from danger and harm. Thankfully, some notable people are willing to put their lives on the line daily and protect people they know and don't know. They are our first responders and members of the military. Everybody needs to show appreciation and respect by thanking them for their service.

HELL: When people arrive in hell, it is too late for them to change their minds and ask God for His protection. Just as they turned their back on God living on Earth, God has turned His back on them in the afterlife. They are eternally separated from the love and protection of God. He does not shield any of them from the curses, punishments, and wrath. Instead, they are coping with ghastly, harmful, and severe consequences they brought on themselves. Everyone desperately needs God, but He is never found here. They are 100% on their own.

Everyone quickly realizes there are no people to support them. Nobody is coming to their rescue and helping them to escape. They are trapped and unable to leave this distressing place. No one is given the strength to cope with the horrendous happenings.

HEAVEN: Everyone belongs to God and Jesus. God protects everybody; therefore, there are no safety issues. Everyone is safe at all times. Heaven is always a win-win situation.

* * * * *

Will you opt <u>not</u> to be protected in hell?
Will you opt to <u>be protected</u> in heaven?

CHAPTER 13

PUNISHMENTS

Even though punishment can be painful and even bring us to tears, it is sometimes necessary. Discipline builds character because it corrects the wrong things found in our personal lives. When punishments are accepted and not rejected, they bring to light valuable lessons to help us grow as individuals.

God thinks character building is critical. He uses our individualized punishments to get our attention. God uses His chisel to remove the bad things in our lives and transform them into beneficial things.

Scripture teaches that God punishes people when needed. His goal is always to get the people back on the right track. For example, in the Book of Amos, God punished the people living in Damascus, Tyre, Edom, Moab, Judah, and Israel, together with the Ammonite people. The punishments came about because God disapproved of their wrong actions, behaviors, and lifestyles.

The Scriptures found in Exodus 7-12 teach that God punished the Egyptians with plagues. The plagues were turning their water into blood, frogs, gnats, swarms of flies, locusts, boils, hail, darkness, and the deaths of their firstborn and livestock. God gave the people plenty of time to acknowledge and ask forgiveness for their sins against Him. Unfortunately, they refused to make the appropriate changes, and as a result of their rebellion, the Egyptians suffered brutal consequences.

Nobody ever takes a day off from sin. All of humanity <u>sins</u> and disobeys God daily. God <u>never</u> sins. He is absolutely corruption free.

HELL: Some people believe there are no punishments here. They feel God will change His mind and lighten up regarding penalties. People think that God will never punish anybody because He is merciful. The mercies that God grants to everyone during their lifetime will immediately disappear in hell. The punishments are permanent and not temporary. Time has run out. It is too late for anybody to confess and ask the forgiveness of their sins. He gives them the punishments they deserve because they rejected Him.

HEAVEN: Sins are non-existent. Punishments are non-existent. Can you imagine these two things disappearing forever? Does it bring a smile to your face?

* * * * *

Will you opt to be <u>severely</u> punished in hell?
Will you opt <u>never</u> to be punished in heaven?

* * * * *

Some parents take their child-raising role very seriously. They control their children, but their children never control them. The parents decide what actions and behaviors are acceptable and not acceptable. When one of their children does something wrong, they are punished.

    A friend of mine told me when she was a child, she was very headstrong and had "selective hearing." Her parents would tell her what she needed to do, but she blew off what they were saying and did her own thing. She specifically remembers one day when her parents told her to go outside and pick out the switch for her punishment. My friend was outside for quite a while but finally came back inside the house with a very small, weak, and bent switch. She felt this switch would cause her no pain. However, her parents disagreed with her choice and sent her back outside to select another switch.

<u>HELL</u>: There are all types of punishments and dreadful consequences. The sentences and the attached results are excruciating and upsetting. Those who turned their backs and rejected God are now suffering from being eternally separated from His love.

<u>HEAVEN</u>: Punishments and attached consequences are non-existent.

* * * * *

Will you opt to <u>endure</u> all types of punishments and consequences in hell?
Will you opt <u>never</u> to endure any punishments or consequences in heaven?

CHAPTER 14
OBEDIENCE

When people obey the leadership, they acknowledge an authority figure and do what they are told. When people are disobedient to leadership, they are defiant and non-compliant. God is obeyed and disobeyed daily. God loves to be followed but hates to be disregarded. The heavenly angels, cherubim, seraphim, sun, moon, sextillion stars, every galaxy and planet, all the bodies of water, and the entire animal kingdom all submit to His authority. None of them ever argue or question God; instead, they obey Him.

HELL: Everybody is here because of their disobedience. They made their personal choice of being disobedient to God. This was one of the worst decisions they made during their lifetime. As a result of their choice, all of them are continuously suffering emotionally, mentally, and physically.

HEAVEN: Everyone personally decided that God was worthy of their obedience. This was the best decision they have ever made. They are greatly rewarded for making the right choice.

* * * * *

Will you opt to <u>refuse</u> to obey God and suffer horrific consequences in hell?

Will you opt to <u>make every effort</u> to obey God and suffer no consequences in heaven?

CHAPTER 15
NO ESCAPE

One day, I thought about not being able to escape a dreadful situation. A sorrowful memory came to my mind. One of my friends was caring, kindhearted, polite, and thoughtful. When we parted ways on a Friday afternoon, we both expected to see each other on Monday morning. That never happened.

Over the weekend, her dwelling burned down, and she could not escape. After reading the facts in the newspaper, I sat down on the kitchen floor and cried. I could not imagine what my friend went through because nobody could help her escape the horror. I was grief-stricken.

Think of being inside a burning building. Inside it is scorching, smoky, and dangerous. It is hard to breathe and impossible to see. You can hear the crackling of the flames. You are trapped, panic-stricken, and desperate to escape.

HELL: It is insufferably hot and dangerous. The atmosphere is of terror and desperation because God and His goodness are nowhere to be found. Everyone is petrified because there is no escape, no help, and no end to their dire situation. Imagine how it would feel to be in this situation:

1. People are all alone.
2. People are trapped, confined, and unable to escape.
3. People are losing it emotionally and mentally because of their entrapment.
4. Nobody can save them.
5. People physically shake because of their entrapment.
6. People are beaten down emotionally, mentally, and physically.

7. All communications are shut down.
8. There is no light, only complete darkness.
9. Smells are disgusting.
10. The temperature is intense and swelteringly hot.
11. People are frantic, high-strung, hyper, hysterical, and stressed.
12. People are going bonkers and becoming basket cases.
13. People cave in and give up.
14. Hope turns into hopelessness.
15. People are forced to cope with their destructive emotions.
16. People lose all control.
17. People are furious and full of rage.
18. People are yelling and screaming at the top of their lungs.
19. People are sobbing, whimpering, and wailing uncontrollably.
20. The place is creepy, eerie, scary, and spooky.
21. People have a hard time accepting the reality of their situation.

HEAVEN: No one ever wants to leave the presence of God.

* * * * *

Will you opt <u>never to</u> be rescued and trapped in hell?
Will you opt never to <u>want</u> to escape heaven?

CHAPTER 16

MAGGOTS AND WORMS

In Mark 9:48, Jesus describes hell as "where the maggots never die and the fire never goes out." A maggot is the larva of a fly and can often be found near rotting food, dead animals, or garbage. They are dirty, grimy, and carry disease. The maggots are slow-moving creepy insects. Their body is slimy and soft.

The Bible warns us there are also worms in hell. Isaiah 66:24 says, "And as they go out, they will see the dead bodies of those who have rebelled against me. For the worms that devour them will never die, and the fire that burns them will never go out. All who pass by will view them with utter horror." This is because the appetites of the larvae and worms are never satisfied. Everybody is constantly being gnawed at and bitten.

I tried to picture maggots underneath me and worms on top of me. Can you imagine? Picture this: You have a custom-built bathtub that fits your body perfectly from your head to your toes. The bottom of the bathtub is filled with slimy maggots. You step into your tub naked and lie down. Next, it is filled to the top with slimy worms. The maggots underneath you start to chew at your body. The worms on top of you are doing the same thing.

You begin to panic. Instantly, you want to escape the awful situation. You soon discover you are unable to lift your head. You cannot move your arms, hands, feet, or legs, so you cannot brush the maggots and worms off you. The worms slowly crawl on your face, in your hair, between your toes, on the tops of your arms, hands, legs, feet, and under your armpits.

You will not want to open your mouth to cry or scream because they will crawl inside your mouth and down your throat. You will want to keep your eyes closed because they will crawl inside your eyes. You will not want to breathe because they will crawl up your nose and slowly move inside your ears. Worms like darkness. The dark areas of your face are inside of your eyes, nose, mouth, throat, and ears. The maggots will crawl on the bottoms of your feet, the back of your legs, arms, hands, and head.

How do you think the maggots and worms would make you feel? Does it gross you out? It does me.

HELL: Nobody can control the overabundance of maggots and worms. Nothing can be done to stop them from slowly crawling all over their bodies. The appetites of the maggots and worms are out-of-control. They are chewing and nibbling non-stop.

HEAVEN: Maggots and worms are non-existent here.

* * * * *

Will you opt to <u>experience</u> an overabundance of maggots and worms in hell?

Will you opt to be <u>free</u> of maggots and worms in heaven?

CHAPTER 17

PARADISE

Imagine yourself boarding an airplane and arriving shortly after on an unforgettable tropical vacation. You are now in paradise. During the day, the weather is delightful with a constant and gentle breeze. You are surrounded by exotic birds, tropical flowers, and trees. You can see your feet in the water and different types of colorful fish because it is so pristine. You can hear and see impressive waterfalls. You are walking on white sand, collecting seashells on the shoreline. The sunrises and sunsets are spectacular.

What are your thoughts about staying at this tropical resort? How do you feel emotionally, mentally, and physically? Do you feel relaxed, as if you have a new lease on life? Do you feel anxious and stressed out? Do you want to leave, or do you want to stay?

HELL: It is not a sought-after paradise; instead, it is a never-ending nightmare. Hell is void of all positivity. Everything found here is 100% negative. This place affects everyone. They are going bonkers, freaking out, and becoming hysterical. It is like being stuck in a pressure cooker ready to explode. Nobody wants to stay in this place because of the unsettling and unstable environment. They want to escape immediately but cannot.

HEAVEN: Think of a paradise you've seen advertised in brochures, magazines, social media, or television. The water, sunsets, sunrises, landscaping, and the different types of birds and fish are very colorful.

Heaven is described as a picture-perfect paradise, and it is incredibly bright. God has given us a glimpse of His use and love of colors on Earth. The colors found on the Earth are no match for the colors found here. The colors displayed all over heaven are stunning. There are colors in heaven that have never been seen on Earth.

No one here is ever stressed or disappointed. On the contrary, everybody feels superb emotionally, mentally, and physically. Everyone is having the best time of their life. Nobody wants to leave, not even for a split second.

* * * * *

Will you opt to live in the <u>non</u>-paradise place in hell?
Will you opt to live in the <u>perfect</u> paradise place in heaven?

CHAPTER 18

REUNIONS OR ISOLATION

A reunion is a great way to connect with family members. It allows us to hear what is happening in the lives of other family members, as well as seeing pictures of their children, grandchildren, great-grandchildren, and pets.

There are two types of reunions. Some reunions are incredibly enjoyable, and they bring smiles to faces. Other reunions are miserable get-togethers. When the reunion is tense, it can bring out deep-seated anger, words that cannot be taken back, and tears. In addition, it can shed light on unresolved issues and long-standing feuds.

HELL: There are no joyous reunions here. People aren't hugging their loved ones and being greeted by familiar faces.

HEAVEN: In 2nd Samuel 12:13-23, the child of David and Bathsheba became very ill. David knew only one person could heal his child, and it was God. He went without food and sleep, praying for a miracle to happen. Unfortunately, the child died. David's advisers were afraid to tell him of the child's death because they were unsure how he would react. After he found out his child had died, David got up, washed his body, changed his clothes, and worshiped God. His advisers were shocked at David's behavior. David's response to them was that he knew he would be reunited with his child one day.

When we arrive in heaven, we are reunited with our family members, friends, acquaintances, and coworkers who are also believers. I have thought about the people I want to connect with when I arrive. I have two brothers I have never met. One brother died within 24 hours of his birth. My other brother died within 48 hours of his birth. I only know their names. I am looking forward to meeting them face-to-face.

* * * * *

Will you opt to be <u>severely lonely</u> because there are no reunions in hell?
Will you opt for <u>thrilling</u> reunions in heaven?

* * * * *

I want you to make a mental list of your family members, friends, acquaintances, and work associates. What do they do for you? What do you expect them to do for you? Do you find yourself being dependent on these people?

People still need others, and this will never change. God purposely wired us for community. Everyone wants to be needed, sought after, and chosen to meet other people's needs.

<u>HELL</u>: People are here because they relied on the wrong things. Many people were dependent solely on their good works or efforts. Others chose to ignore God instead of embracing Him. Some even followed false spiritual leaders and their affiliated religions. As a result of their misplaced reliance, they are now isolated from the people they desperately need. Everyone is contending with extreme loneliness and isolation from other people.

<u>HEAVEN</u>: Everyone depended solely on God. They accepted the gift of eternal life through Jesus, who paid for all of their sins. Nobody relied on themselves, spiritual leaders, or

Reunions or Isolation

religions. No one is ever isolated from God, Jesus, heavenly beings, and other believers. Loneliness is non-existent.

* * * * *

Will you <u>always opt</u> to be isolated from all the people in hell? Will you opt <u>never</u> to be isolated in heaven?

CHAPTER 19
NO COMMUNICATION

I once lived in a big city with a large, diverse population. Some of the English-speaking residents would say to the non-native speakers, "You are in my country now, so speak our language." Hearing another language greatly offended them because they could not understand the words. They became annoyed, unkind, and unsympathetic towards those who could not speak English well. There were often misunderstandings for those who did try to understand them without a common language. Communication barriers can cause people to have negative interactions with others.

In Genesis 11:1-9, we read about the Tower of Babel. The people decided to build a city and a tower extending to the heavens. They thought this goal was attainable. God became very displeased with their decision. At that time, everybody spoke the same language, but that abruptly ended. God scattered them all over the world. He made everyone speak different languages.

HELL: People are not sitting around chatting, sharing ideas, and swapping funny stories.

HEAVEN: It is an international melting pot, and it is an exciting place. There are people from all over the world, and there are no language barriers. The people either speak the same language or are able to speak and understand all the different languages.

Stop and think about the exciting conversations you will have with people from all over the world. Also, can you

No Communication

imagine sitting down and personally talking with Mary, Esther, Eve, David, Job, Noah, and others? We are going to see them and have the opportunity to speak with all of them if we so desire.

* * * * *

Will you opt for <u>no communication</u> with other people in hell? Will you opt for <u>communication</u> with all of the people in heaven?

CHAPTER 20

NO WATER

When you are hot and sweating, what do you want? Do you walk into your kitchen and open your refrigerator looking for something to drink? Water is more important than food. It is very precious and priceless when trying to survive.

One day, I thought about being exceedingly thirsty. God brought to my mind people in a desert. The sun is brightly shining. The temperature is boiling and oppressive. There is no shade. Everybody is downcast and physically exhausted. Walking is almost impossible, even though they slowly put one foot in front of the other. The lack of water is becoming life-threatening. They are ever so desperate to find water, but there is nothing to quench their endless thirst.

HELL: On Earth, water is readily available to most of us. But in hell, tap water, bottled water, ice cubes, water fountains, and water hoses are non-existent. Everybody is constantly searching for something to drink because they are incredibly thirsty. Yet their request to obtain water is continually denied. Nobody is given anything to quench their dire thirst, cool off their tongue, or alleviate their dry throat. They are in urgent need of relief and are incredibly dehydrated.

Remember the lesson Jesus taught about Lazarus and the rich man? The rich man who is in hell asked someone to dip their finger in some water to cool off his tongue. His request was flat-out denied. Nothing has changed for the rich man. His thirst has never been quenched.

No Water

HEAVEN: The people are never thirsty because their every need is met.

* * * * *

Will you opt to be <u>constantly</u> thirsty in hell?
Will you opt to <u>never</u> be thirsty in heaven?

CHAPTER 21

SEPARATION FROM GOD

I have heard that the most stressful events many of us will experience are the death of a spouse, divorce, significant injury or illness, moving, and job loss. All these events involve losing or being separated from the things important to us – our spouse, home, community, livelihood, and health. These significant life changes tear us away from things that are comfortable and familiar to us and plunge us into the unknown.

As I thought about being alone and separated from the familiar, God brought the following image to mind. You are in the middle of the ocean. The sun is brightly shining, a warm breeze is blowing, and the waves are very gentle. You are the captain of a brand-new fishing boat. There are no crew members on board yet because you are on your way to pick them up and begin a month-long fishing trip.

Within a few hours, you receive alerts regarding a massive storm brewing nearby. You start to read the electronic information and listen to the radio transmissions of nearby ships. Suddenly, your boat loses power, and you can no longer receive the desperately needed communications. Without power, the entire boat plunges into darkness. There are very few stars in the sky, and the sliver of moon barely gives off any light. You are on your own, isolated, and without help. Within a short time, you find yourself in the middle of a developing and threatening storm.

You lose total control of the steering mechanism because of mechanical problems. You cannot fix or jerry-rig any of the issues temporarily or permanently. The waves are now immense.

Separation from God

They keep pounding the entire boat non-stop with their powerful force. The mammoth waves are overtaking the boat.

You fly out of your captain's seat and end up on the floor, thrown around violently. You are severely injured and desperately need medical attention. As a result of the power outage, you cannot call for help and are isolated. The boat rocks back and forth violently in the giant swells.

You become panic-stricken. You begin to think and quietly ask yourself questions: Am I going to die all alone in the middle of the ocean? Will I ever see my loved ones again? What have I done to deserve this?

HELL: For many of us, when everything is going well in our life, God is the last person that we think about. When our lives unexpectedly fall apart, we quickly look for God. We instantly want God's help to get us through our darkest days. Many call on Him the most when times are devastating, grueling, and tragic.

God is never found in hell. Being there means eternal and irreversible separation from His love and protection. The last person you want to become divorced and disconnected from is God because it leads to an eternity of unleashed judgment, punishment, and wrath.

HEAVEN: No divorce papers are served here. God never divorces Himself from anybody in heaven. He takes care of everyone and meets all of their needs.

* * * * *

Will you opt to be divorced from God?

* * * * *

When people die, they immediately enter the afterlife. They are never physically seen again on Earth. God is not the God of the dead but the living. Everyone is very much alive in both heaven and hell. Death is non-existent in both locations.

HELL: Everybody is separated from God forever because of their personal choice. Their wrong choice has dire consequences attached. The results the people are dealing with, at this very moment, are God's severe curses and punishments.

HEAVEN: Nobody is separated from God. He is always with them. Therefore, curses and punishments are non-existent.

* * * * *

Will you opt to be <u>separated</u> from God in hell forever?
Will you opt <u>never to be separated</u> from God in heaven?

CHAPTER 22
DESPERATION

One day, I had an appointment to see my eye specialist. While I waited, I looked at the eye chart on the wall. I immediately noticed the first line on the eye chart was huge and easily seen. The last line on the eye chart was tiny and almost impossible to read. I realized that God is like the first line on the eye chart. All the negative things happening to me are like the letters on the last line of the eye chart. I reminded myself that God is more significant than my desperation. My adverse circumstances are minuscule compared to the living God's enormity.

When I think about the eye chart, it helps me to put things in the proper perspective. It allows me to control my emotions and feelings and not let them have persuasive power over me.

HELL: People are very desperate to leave. They are scared out of their wits, highly stressed, and panic-stricken. No one is coming to rescue them or put an end to their dreadful situation. Their desperation will continue for eternity.

HEAVEN: Nobody is desperate. Everybody is at ease, stress-free, and tranquil because they are with God.

* * * * *

Will you opt to be desperate in hell <u>constantly</u>?
Will you opt <u>never</u> to be desperate in heaven?

CHAPTER 23
OPTIMIST VS. PESSIMIST

We are either an optimist or a pessimist. An optimist sees the glass of water as half full. The pessimist sees the same glass of water as being half empty.

Optimistic people appear to be the happiest. They are usually very upbeat, filled with excitement, hopeful, and think and talk about their future. Optimists are bright rays of sunshine. People have difficulty staying depressed and down in the dumps around them. Optimistic people make others feel good, bringing a smile, not a frown.

Pessimistic people appear to be unhappy. They seem to find and focus on more negative things than positive things regarding their own life and the lives of others. Pessimistic people are dark and gloomy clouds. Some people deliberately avoid pessimism because it brings them down emotionally and mentally.

Unfortunately, none of us have a perfect track record of being optimists or pessimists 100% of the time, tending to waffle back and forth. All of us should try to be rays of sunshine, not dark and gloomy clouds. We all need to choose to be an optimist over a pessimist daily.

What is your personal preference? Do you prefer to be around an optimistic or a pessimistic person?

* * * * *

We may feel hopeful or hopeless when we focus on our future. However, hope gives people an expectation that things will work out, even during the challenging, trying, and painful times. Also, sharing hope encourages the recipient to keep pressing forward despite the circumstances. This is a great thing to experience.

HELL: What do the optimistic people shortly discover regarding their future? It is not delightful; instead, it is very tragic. The optimistic people, who are usually perky and full of life, turn into pessimistic people within a few moments. The reality regarding their harrowing future slaps them very hard in the face.

I thought about how people might feel in hell. Finally, I came up with this list: agitated, annoyed, awful, beaten down, betrayed, bewildered, bitter, bored, dejected, desperate, devastated, distressed, forgotten, frazzled, hated, helpless, ill at ease, infuriated, insignificant, isolated, misled, neglected, overwrought, perplexed, scared, trapped, unloved, vulnerable, and unwelcomed.

Everyone has a dire future ahead of them. Their hope turns into despair, disappointment, and bitter sadness as they realize their circumstances will never improve. It is the ultimate hopeless place.

HEAVEN: Everyone found here is optimistic because they are filled to the brim with hope. Everybody is bubbly and cheery because of their sensational surroundings. I thought about the feelings being experienced, and came up with my laundry list: amazing, blessed, carefree, contented, enthusiastic, fantastic, fearless, healthy, hopeful, joyful, safe, stress-free, thankful, tranquil, treasured, upbeat, wanted, and welcomed.

* * * * *

Will you be an <u>unhappy pessimist</u> because of the hopelessness found in hell?
Will you be an <u>ecstatic optimist</u> because of the hope found in heaven?

CHAPTER 24

REHAB AND HELL

I had an accident and spent 12 hours in the emergency room. Afterward, I was admitted to the hospital for two weeks and sent to a physical rehab facility for several weeks.

Upon my arrival at the rehab facility, I became very discouraged. Within a short time, I was forced to make a decision. I was going to feel sorry for myself or make the best out of a lousy situation. I chose the latter. I made it a point to change my attitude and behavior. I focused on the other patients. I encouraged them, listened to what they were telling me about themselves, and made them laugh.

One day, I told my friend what I was hearing and seeing at the facility. She told me she could see the similarities between the rehab facility and hell. I thought about it, and she was spot-on.

At the rehab facility, I heard the other injured patients, at all different hours, cursing, crying, screaming, and yelling. Some were begging to leave the facility, shouting at the staff members, and being abusive towards their caregivers. Some patients were hollering at their family members, even physically hitting them. They refused physical therapy because of the pain and demanded medication to help them sleep. Some patients had small alarms strapped to their bodies to prevent them from leaving their room. Unfortunately, it wasn't quiet at night, causing many of us to lose sleep. In the morning, there were nasty stenches coming from the laundry room.

Numerous people told me they felt their family and friends had abandoned and forgotten about them. They yearned for encouragement and comfort during this challenging time. I saw the different losses, including their dignity, decision-making ability, health, income, jobs, and insurance coverage.

When I brought up God in my conversations, some people told me they believe a higher power exists. Other people refused to acknowledge and accept God as the higher power. A few people told me they did not believe in God. Several people had no interest in spiritual matters.

Some people told me they were so scared because they could fall and physically reinjure themselves. When I looked at the people directly in their eyes, I saw anger, boredom, depression, fear, frustration, hopelessness, rage, sadness, sleep deprivation, stress, and tears. The rehab facility stay was only temporary and not permanent.

<u>HELL</u>: People are wailing, screaming, yelling, and cursing non-stop. There are high-pitched, ear-piercing noises. The punishments are off-the-chart. There are stomach-turning smells in the whole place. Nobody wants to stay here. Everyone is permanently trapped, and they are unable to leave the premises. Everybody has lost all control over themselves and their environment. Everyone feels like they have been forgotten about and abandoned. Some of the things they are dealing with are anger, depression, fear, frustration, hopelessness, isolation, and stress. Unfortunately, no medications are here to help them successfully cope with their feelings.

Some people here believed God existed, but He was not the higher power. Others decided to reject and turn their back on Him. Some relied exclusively on their chosen false spiritual leader and the religion they represented; others wanted nothing to do with God or spiritual matters.

Nobody expected to arrive here. Now they are being forced to cope with emotional, mental, and physical sufferings, and coming to grips with the cruel reality that their life has permanently changed for the worst. There is no temporary or permanent relief available.

HEAVEN: Many who have endured physical therapy for a long time call it the "torture chamber." Heaven is not a torture chamber. It is permanently 100% painless.

* * * * *

Will you opt to be forced to deal with the <u>dire reality</u> in hell? Will you opt to enjoy the <u>wonderful reality</u> in heaven?

* * * * *

At some point in our lives, we all encounter a health problem or bodily injury. Our bodies are defective. They break down in all different ways that require medical treatment. Some health problems are quickly brought under control, while others will linger on for hours, days, weeks, months, or even years.

HELL: There are no hospitals or clinics where you can receive medical treatment. Everyone has cursed and imperfect eternal bodies.

HEAVEN: Nobody here is ever sick, suffers from diseases or illnesses, sustains injuries, or has disabilities and handicaps. Everybody was immediately healed and permanently released from these things upon their arrival. Everyone has a beautiful, healthy, and flawless eternal body. Their eternal body never breaks down, needs healing, gets old, or lacks energy. There are no hospitals or clinics because the people are 100% healthy.

* * * * *

Will you opt to have an <u>imperfect and cursed</u> eternal body in hell? Will you opt to have a <u>perfect and blessed</u> eternal body in heaven?

CHAPTER 25
DEPENDENCY

Most of us like to be independent, but sometimes we must depend on others. For example, one Saturday morning, I had to run errands. I got into my vehicle and turned the key, but the battery died. I called a friend of mine and told her what had happened. She volunteered to drive me to different places, so I could get my errands done. My friend told me that even though it was irritating, God was in complete control. She kept telling me that, for some reason, God did not want me driving that day.

Later that day, I called my insurance company roadside assistance. They dispatched a tow truck company to come to my home and jump my battery. I became dependent on one of their employees to get my vehicle running once again.

HELL: Everybody is here because they depended on the wrong things. Perhaps they depended solely on themselves and their good works to get them into heaven. Others relied on false spiritual leaders and their affiliated religions to keep them out of this place. Numerous people believed the lie that hell is not real. All of their beliefs were wrong. At this very moment, they are being greatly punished and coping with the appalling consequences of their choice.

HEAVEN: Everyone put their complete dependency on Jesus dying on the cross for their sins. They depended solely on God giving them the gift of salvation. Everybody made the right choice.

* * * * *

Will you depend on the <u>wrong</u> things and land in hell?
Will you depend on the <u>right</u> things and land in heaven?

CHAPTER 26

TOTAL DARKNESS

On a beautiful, warm fall day, I went to a cavern with a friend. Once inside the cavern, our tour guide told us they would turn out all the lights. When they did, I couldn't see anything, not even the hand in front of my face. I could hear what those around me were saying, but I couldn't even make out the outline of a person. Sitting in the complete darkness, I felt defenseless and uncomfortable, like I was an easy target for someone to harm me physically. It wasn't until the lights came back on that I realized I'd been anxiously holding my breath.

When some people are alone, or in complete darkness, in an unknown place, they become very apprehensive. They may feel abandoned. They may even feel at risk, disturbed, ill at ease, stressed out, and vulnerable. They might physically tremble.

HELL: There is no sun, moon, or shining stars. No windows, skylights, electricity, battery-operated lamps and light fixtures, nightlights, flashlights, lighters, candles, or streetlights. What is <u>found</u> here? The darkness is so deep that it can be felt. Nobody ever sees any light whatsoever. The lack of even a glimmer of light significantly impacts everyone emotionally, mentally, and physically.

To spend eternity in hell is to experience impenetrable darkness without end.

HEAVEN: The people see all the exquisite beauty and vivid colors because it is always very luminous.

Total Darkness

Will you opt for <u>complete and intense</u> darkness found in hell?

Will you opt for <u>radiant</u> light found in heaven?

* * * * *

When most people walk into a dark dwelling, they instantly turn on the lights. This action protects them from things they are seeking to avoid.

Everyone has the opportunity to tap into the most critical light. This light is the only true beacon. A beacon gives comfort, encouragement, guidance, hope, support, and warnings. God is the perfect beacon.

When your life appears to be falling apart and you become desperate, you need to seek out God. He is available to help you 24 hours daily to get you through your bleakest, darkest, and most overwhelming days.

God is <u>never</u> found in hell. There is no beacon of light. The people become discouraged, helpless, and hopeless because of their never-ending desperation.

* * * * *

Will you opt to have <u>no</u> beacon of light?

Will you opt to <u>align</u> yourself with the true beacon of light?

CHAPTER 27
MUSIC

Do you find music relaxing and a stress reliever? Do you enjoy going to concerts? Do you zone out when you listen to your favorite tunes or do you rock on? Do other drivers find you entertaining when they catch you flinging your arms side-to-side and up and down as you sing in your vehicle? Do you belt out a song at the top of your lungs? Can your radio be heard by other drivers with their windows up because the volume is so high?

How important is music to you? Can you go a day without music? Some types of music are very calming. Other types of music set in motion different feelings.

HELL: Music would be advantageous here because the people are so troubled. It would help everybody to calm down. Unfortunately, there are no musical instruments or joyous sounds here. Instead, the people vocalize their excruciating emotional, mental, and physical sufferings. The sound of their anguish is deafening and endless.

HEAVEN: God is the creator of music. The Bible encourages us to worship Him with instruments. In Psalm 150:4, the psalmist says, "Praise Him with tambourine and dancing; praise Him with strings and flutes!"

God may be the last person most people picture singing and playing every musical instrument. Scripture says He sings. In Zephaniah 3:17, we read "He will rejoice over you with joyful songs." How do you think His voice sounds? Can you imagine hearing God singing flawlessly and playing every type of musical instrument faultlessly?

Music

There are music and musical instruments found here. The different types of music bring joy and cause everybody to feel tranquil and relaxed. God is not monotonous. He is far from being humdrum. God loves variety. He wants everybody to appreciate and enjoy all types of music, not just one.

The Bible says God expected the people to praise Him using their flutes, harps, lyres, strings, tambourines, trumpets, and loud clanging cymbals, together with dancing. The music during these times was energetic, exciting, lively, and loud. This confirms God loves loud noises and not hushed and motionless praise and worship.

* * * * *

Will you opt <u>never</u> to hear any music or musical instruments in hell?

Will you opt to <u>hear</u> a variety of music and musical instruments in heaven?

CHAPTER 28

LAUGHTER

Has the sound of someone else's laughter ever made you laugh? Laughter is a great thing. When people laugh, it causes other people around them to smile and laugh, even those who are feeling down. Laughing is a stress reliever and is very beneficial health-wise. I have been told it takes fewer muscles to laugh than to frown.

<u>HELL</u>: Nobody laughs because nothing funny ever happens. Instead, there is only pain, turmoil, and endless regret.

<u>HEAVEN</u>: Do you think God views laughter as being important? Do you believe God has a sense of humor? We know from Genesis that He made man in His image, so it isn't hard to imagine that God enjoys amusement just as we do. God has given everyone a unique laugh and a sense of humor. He wants us to use them!

Since all good things are found in heaven, there will be laughter, joy, and amusement. So be prepared to flash your pearly whites!

* * * * *

Will you opt to <u>frown and never laugh</u> in hell?
Will you opt to <u>laugh and never frown</u> in heaven?

* * * * *

We need to incorporate laughter into our lives daily. Ask God to give you something to laugh about every day. Here are some things that have brought a big smile to my face.

1. A friend's dog goes to Doggie Day Care. The owner told my friend that her dog has <u>numerous</u> boyfriends (no

girlfriends). She is known as the Cougar. She is 12 years old, but her boyfriends' ages range from two to six. She flat-out refuses to play with any of the old geezers.
2. Two ducks stopped heavy traffic. I watched them slowly stroll across the busy street, utterly unconcerned about all those stopped cars. No, they were not in the crosswalk.
3. An owner and their dog went into the bank to make a deposit. The dog came out of the bank carrying the empty deposit bag in its mouth. He was enormously proud of his performance and had a big smile. The dog quickly jumped into the owner's car and was strapped into his seatbelt.
4. A good friend of mine went to the hospital to have lunch with her sister. They had planned to meet in the cafeteria at noon. My friend got on the elevator in the hospital lobby and pressed a button. When the elevator stopped, she got off and walked down a long and dimly lit hallway. Instead of walking into the cafeteria, she walked into the morgue. She told me she became so frazzled that she could not remember how to get out of there.

Do yourself a favor. Smile and not frown. Laugh and never stop laughing.

CHAPTER 29
THE BEST HOME

Imagine this scenario. A home builder with a solid reputation will give away a well-built and beautiful new brick home. The offer is free with no hidden costs. The house has a large kitchen with an island and granite countertops, a breakfast nook, and all the best high-end appliances. In addition, there is a dining room, living room, family room, game room, reading room, craft room, office, and laundry room. The main bedroom has a sitting room and an ensuite bathroom. There are seven other large bedrooms, all with walk-in closets. The home also features hardwood floors, four fireplaces, skylights, solar panels, central heat and air, and wired for the fastest internet and cable available. There is also a large double deck with a fire pit, a separate pool house with a hot tub, a five-car garage, a circular driveway, a large gardening shed, and a fenced-in backyard.

The house is situated on 10 acres. The property is simply breathtaking. The trees are over 100 years old. As a nice perk, the home builder will include the services of a groundskeeper who will take care of the lawn maintenance. Additionally, the house is in a great part of town—the best school district, within five miles of the city, and the crime rate is zero.

The home builder is handing over the deed and the keys to the winner of the giveaway. Sounds idyllic, right?

Now picture this instead. Another contest is giving away an old and used cardboard box. This box is in a dangerous inner-city alley behind smelly dumpsters. Rats, maggots, mice, roaches, snakes, and slimy worms live around the box.

The Best Home

This cardboard box does not protect from the weather or anything else. The city has sweltering and humid days during the summer and heavy snowfall, blizzards, ice, bone-chilling temperatures, and blustery winds during the winter. The spring and fall seasons only last for a month or less.

This specific alley is a focal point of criminal activity. The criminals in the area are entertained by severely hurting the people living in the cardboard boxes. Receiving any help is virtually impossible because of the dangerous environment and the out-of-control violence.

If you were given a choice, what would be your preference? Choosing to be given the deed and the keys to the beautiful house? Or living in the old and used cardboard box?

* * * * *

Will you opt to be the recipient of the <u>grisly</u> cardboard box in hell?
Will you opt to be the recipient of the <u>spectacular</u> home in heaven?

* * * * *

One day, I thought about why people have difficulty expressing anticipation and excitement about their future home in heaven. It might be because of the never-ending challenges that life doles out. Perhaps people have a tough time focusing on the future when they struggle to get through the day. Yet, God wants us to embrace the future hope that is found in heaven. He expects all of us to show our eagerness.

Here are just a few things awaiting us in our heavenly home:

- ▶ There will be <u>no</u> more deaths, disabilities, diseases, handicaps, illnesses, sickness, sins, emotional, mental, and physical pains and sufferings.

Where is Your Eternal Destiny

- ▶ All these things are non-existent: anger, arguments, broken hearts, crying, weeping, wailing, depression, despondency, disagreements, disappointments, discouragement, entrapment, envy and jealousy, farewells, fears, hatred, heartaches, homelessness, hopelessness, loneliness, minor and major losses, meanness, meltdowns, mourning, personality conflicts, phobias, prejudices, pressures, profanity, racism, rejection, revenge, stress, sorrows, struggles, temptations, troubles, trials, tribulations, and worries.
- ▶ No abuse of people and animals.
- ▶ No pornography, sexual abuse, human trafficking, corruption, crimes, threats, violence, drive-by shootings, kidnappings, killings, suicides, bullies, people purposely injuring others, terrorists, gangs, distinct types of hate, racist, and supremacist groups, persecutions, tyrannies, chaos, destruction, devastation, tragedies, traumas, natural disasters, chemical warfare, nuclear threats, and deadly wars.
- ▶ I am saving the best for last of what will <u>not</u> be found. <u>No</u> Satan. <u>No</u> demons.

Everyone will be permanently released from all of the things mentioned above. Everything will disappear, be gone forever, and never be dealt with again.

＊ ＊ ＊ ＊ ＊

Will you opt to be <u>concerned</u> about the future home awaiting in hell?
Will you opt to be <u>enthusiastic</u> about the future home awaiting in heaven?

CHAPTER 30
QUALITY OR NO QUALITY

While walking in the park one day, a bicyclist stopped beside me, and we started talking. He told me he was under tremendous stress. The young man told me if he could not ride his bike 10-12 miles every day, he would have no quality of life. One day, I thought about what it means to have a good quality of life. A good quality of life is possible when people are given freedoms, allowed to make personal choices, and have access to outlets to relieve stress.

<u>HELL</u>: There is no quality of life. Life is arduous.

<u>HEAVEN</u>: Disenchantment does not exist because the picture-perfect quality of life is found here and nowhere else.

* * * * *

Will you opt to have <u>no</u> quality of life in hell?
Will you opt to <u>have</u> quality of life in heaven?

* * * * *

Do you act like a dog and explore and discover your surroundings? Are you curious as a cat about your environment? Do you prefer freedom or <u>no</u> freedom to explore? Do you like being given the chance to discover new things or <u>no</u> chance to discover any new thing?

<u>HELL</u>: Everyone is deprived of things that would help them emotionally, mentally, and physically. Everybody is refused chances to discover, explore, and move around freely.

HEAVEN: People are permitted to freely move around, allowing them to explore and discover unknown things. God expects everybody to look, find, and enjoy their stunning surroundings.

*****

Will you opt to be <u>denied</u> discovering, exploring, and moving around in hell?

Will you opt to be <u>permitted</u> to discover, explore, and move around in heaven?

CHAPTER 31

TWO BASKETS

Many people will comparison shop to get the most value for their money. When comparing prices, the majority of people will compare prices for food, clothes, shoes, housing, vehicles, technology, the best place to get their education, as well as countless other products and services. Everyone wants to get the most they can for their money.

The afterlife is the most crucial thing to comparison shop. Envision going to the local store and comparison shopping between heaven and hell. I want you to grab your imaginary shopping cart with the two baskets inside of the cart. One basket is labeled "No Pains," and the other basket is labeled "Never-Ending Sufferings." After completing your comparison shopping, go to the cashier and give them the imaginary basket you wish to purchase. The "No Pains" basket is green, and the "Never-Ending Sufferings" basket is red.

NO PAINS COLUMN	**NEVER-ENDING SUFFERINGS COLUMN**
ATTRIBUTES OF GOD	
Heaven	**Hell**
Gentle, good, encouraging, kind, nice, and loving	God is never found here
Welcomes everyone	God is never found here
Greets everybody	God is never found here

Accepts everyone	God is never found here
Cares for everybody	God is never found here
Encourages everyone	God is never found here
Loves everybody	God is never found here
Meets the needs of everyone	God is never found here
Talks to everybody	God is never found here
Laughs	God is never found here
Smiles	God is never found here
Teaches	God is never found here
Sings	God is never found here
Plays musical instruments	God is never found here

FOUND AND NOT FOUND

Heaven	Hell
God	No God
Jesus	No Jesus
Angels, cherubim, and seraphim	No heavenly beings
Optimists	Pessimists
People with confessed sins	People with non-confessed sins
People with forgiven sins	People with non-forgiven sins

COMMON DENOMINATORS

Heaven	Hell
Alert People	Alert People
Alive People	Alive People
Awake People	Awake People
Conscious People	Conscious People
Surrounding awareness	Surrounding awareness
Eternal bodies	Eternal bodies
Souls	Souls

Spirits   Spirits
Nobody will physically die   Nobody will physically die

POPULATION

Heaven   **Hell**
Under-populated   Overpopulated

HANDED OUT

Heaven   **Hell**
Blessings   Curses
Rewards   Punishments

FOUND AND NOT FOUND

Heaven	**Hell**
Mansions	No mansions
Gold streets	Hewn stones
Gems	No gems
Jewels	No jewels
Pearls	No pearls
Gates open 24 hours per day	Gates locked 24 hours per day
No burning	Everlasting burning
No burning coals	Fiery coals
No brimstone	Raining brimstone
No fires	Literal fires
No fire pits	Fire pits
No smoke	Thick and very dark smoke
No locusts	Locusts
No nauseating smells	Stomach-turning smells
No sulfur smells	Abundance of sulfur smells

Banquets	No banquets
Celebrations	No celebrations
Festivals	No festivals
Parties	No parties

RELIGIONS AND RELIGIOUS LEADERS

Heaven	**Hell**
Religion free	Different types of false religions
No religious leaders	Slews of false religious leaders

ENVIRONMENT

Heaven	**Hell**
Paradise	Nightmare
Amazing	Unremarkable
Fabulous	Atrocious
Mind-blowing	Mind-numbing
Beautiful	Ugly
Colorful	Colorless
Activities	Activities are non-existent
Fun-filled	No fun
Interesting	Boring
Light	Intense darkness that is felt
Perfect	Imperfect
Positive	Negative
Calm	Frantic
Safe	Dangerous
Stable	Volatile
No tragedies	Catastrophes
No violence	Violent

INTERACTIONS

Heaven	Hell
Talking with God	No God
Talking with Jesus	No Jesus
Talking with the heavenly beings	No heavenly beings
Talking with people from around the world	Complete Isolation from everyone
Reunions	No reunions

TEMPERATURES AND HEAT

Heaven	Hell
Perfect temperatures	Scorching temperatures
Ideal heat	Extreme and excruciating heat
Soft blowing cool breezes	Scorching winds

PERFECTIONS AND IMPERFECTIONS

Heaven	Hell
Perfect eternal body	Imperfect eternal body
Perfect emotional health	Major emotional deficiencies
Perfect mental health	Major mental deficiencies
Perfect physical health	Major health deficiencies

POSITIVE AND NEGATIVE THINGS FOUND

Heaven	Hell
Names found in the Book of Life	Names not found in the Book of Life
Quality of life	No quality of life

Quiet moments	Deafening moments
Personal desires fulfilled	Unfilled desires
All expectations exceeded	Expectations are unmet
Enjoying life	Hating life
Communicating with an array of people	No communicating with anybody
Discovering and exploring new things	No discovering or exploring anything
Learning	No learning anything
Laughing	Crying
Smiling	Frowning
Working	Never working
Listening to all types of music	Vocalizing pains and suffering
Participating in fun and exciting activities	No participating in anything

GOOD AND BAD

Heaven	**Hell**
Accepted	Rejected
Blessed	Cursed
Bliss	Misery
Calm	Turbulent
Carefree	Troubled
Cherished	Neglected
Comfortable	Uncomfortable
Composed	Flustered
Content	Dissatisfied
Easy going	Uptight
Encouraged	Discouraged
Energetic	Lethargic
Enjoyment	Unhappiness

Two Baskets

Excited	Bored
Exuberant	Unexcited
Fearless	Fearful
Forgiven	Never forgiven
Freedom	Trapped
God's control	Out-of-Control
God's order	Disorder
God's delight	Displeasure
God's kindness	Cruelty
Protected	Vulnerable
Guiltless	Guilty
Happy	Unhappy
Hopeful	Hopeless
Important	Insignificant
Joyful	Gloomy
Jubilant	Joyless
Laid back	High strung
Loved	Hated
Peaceful	Peaceless
Protected	Unprotected
Respected	Disrespected
Safe	Unsafe
Satisfied	Unsatisfied
Secure	At risk
Serene	Agitated
Shameless	Ashamed
Significant	Insignificant
Strong	Weak
Supported	Abandoned
Tranquil	Upset
Stress-free	Stressful
Unafraid	Scared to death

Undisturbed	At the end of your rope
Unruffled	Edgy
Unworried	Basket case
Victor	Victim
Vigorous	Listless
Wanted	Never wanted
Welcomed	Never welcomed
Winner	Loser

"NO" LIST

Heaven	**Hell**
No abuse	Very abusive
No agony	Non-stop agony
No anger	God's unleashed anger
No anguish	Pain and suffering
No disturbing things	Distressing things
No chaos	Chaotic
No concerns	Non-stop concerns
No confinement	Being trapped at all times
No depression	Severe and lasting depression
No desire to die	No desire to live
No desire to escape	No desire to stay
No devastation	Very destructive
No discouragement	No encouragement
No evil	Evil
No fears	Terrors
No fright	Fright
No gnashing of teeth	Non-stop gnashing of teeth
No guilt	Guilt-ridden
No hatred	No love
No horror	Shocking

Two Baskets

No hunger	Hungry
No idleness	Listlessness
No isolation	Complete isolation
No loneliness	Loneliness
No maggots and worms	Maggots and worms eating people
No medications needed	No medications available
No nakedness	Nakedness
No physical death	No physical death
No physical pains	Acute physical pains
No pressures	Pressure filled
No problems	Non-stop problems
No rage	Rage
No sadness	Gloominess
No sins	Sinful
No sorrows	Non-stop sorrows
No stress	Stressful
No sufferings	Non-stop sufferings
No tears	Non-stop crying, weeping, and wailing
No terrors	Non-stop terrors
No thirst	Unquenchable thirst
No torments or tortures	Non-stop torments and tortures
No concerns, troubles, or worries	Non-stop concerns, troubles, and worries
No violence	Violent
No viciousness	Vicious
No weakness	No strength
No wickedness	Wicked

* * * * *

Where is Your Eternal Destiny

What basket are you choosing?

* * * * *

Will you opt for the <u>red basket</u>, "Never Ending Sufferings" found in hell?
Will you opt for the <u>green basket</u>, "No Pains" found in heaven?

CHAPTER 32

ENEMIES

All of us have both friends and enemies. A friend is very accepting and treats us well. An enemy will scheme and devise a plan of how to attack and destroy their opponent. The enemy will deliberately harm their opponent emotionally, mentally, and physically. They have no intentions of becoming their friend.

When people become hurt, they will either choose to retaliate or not. Retaliation causes bad outcomes, unleashing anger, hatred, and revenge towards the other person. When we decide not to get even, we are free from anger, hatred, and revenge.

God disapproves of retaliation. He wants to take care of the situation. In Romans 12:19, Paul writes, "Dear friends, never take revenge. Leave that to the righteous anger of God. The Scriptures say, 'I will take revenge; I will pay them back,' says the Lord." We should hand the situation over to God to take care of because He is the ultimate expert. Then move forward with your life.

Jesus had enemies. He was forced to decide to retaliate or not against His enemies. I want you to think about Jesus before He died on the cross. Who were His enemies? One was Judas, who was His friend that betrayed Him. Then there were the authority figures who falsely accused Him, imprisoned Him, and permitted unfair and illegal hearings and trials to be brought against Him. There were also the soldiers who ruthlessly hurt Him. Finally, a large crowd of people demanded Jesus be placed on a cross to die.

Jesus could have easily called on thousands of angels to come to His rescue and snuff out the lives of His enemies.

Instead, Jesus did three incredible things. First, He chose not to retaliate against any of His enemies. Then Jesus asked God to forgive all of them. Finally, He went a step further and died an abysmal death on the cross for all their sins.

God has enemies. They rebel against Him, disrespect Him, ignore Him, refuse to listen to Him, disobey Him, say nasty things, shake their fists, turn their backs, and reject Him.

There are two groups of sinners. Neither one of these groups of people takes a day off from sin. What grouping do you fall into? Group 1 or Group 2?

Group 1 – After sinning, this group of people will try to do the right thing. They will acknowledge what they did was wrong, ask God for His forgiveness, make every effort to alter their behavior and seek His approval.

God considers this group His children. He acts like a loving parent and disciplines them if necessary. I have noticed when I blow it on a particular day, God does not punish me. Instead, He favors me and allows good things to happen. His approach pulls me in line very quickly.

Every time we sin, we are God's temporary enemies. When we die, we will not die as an enemy of God because of His forgiveness of all our sins.

Group 2 – This group of people refuses to acknowledge and ask for the forgiveness of their sins. They reject the idea of doing their utmost to change their wrong actions and behaviors. God does not retaliate against this group of people while living on Earth. Instead, He gives them countless opportunities to change their mindset and behaviors. Unfortunately, these chances end abruptly, upon their death, and they die as His enemy.

HELL: All of the people found in Group 2 are God's enemies. They are here because they rejected Him, turned their backs on

Him, and wanted nothing to do with Him. Upon their arrival, their traumatic journey just begins because God retaliates against them. He forces them to endure His unleashed anger, rage, and wrath. At this very moment, they are enduring atrocious punishments and sufferings that will surpass trillions of years.

HEAVEN: Those found in Group 1 are not enemies of God. On the contrary, they are children of God, and He is still their loving Father.

* * * * *

Will you opt to end up in hell and <u>endure</u> all of God's retaliation?
Will you opt to end up in heaven and <u>never endure</u> God's retaliation?

CHAPTER 33

JUDGMENT

When a person is judged, they are held accountable for their actions. People brought up on criminal charges appear before a judge. The judge will either give them a lenient or harsh sentence they must serve. At all times, the judge has the final say and not the offender.

All of us, at one time or another, have acted arrogantly towards God. We may have blamed Him for things that happened or did not happen in our lives.

1. God did not answer our prayers the way we expected.
2. We feel He deliberately turned His back on us or that He abandoned or forgot about us.
3. We feel He did the wrong things, making us suffer needlessly, picking on us, purposely pushing us to our breaking point, not giving us breaks we desperately needed, and not turning a bad situation into a good one.

Such arrogance towards God is wrong. We should never judge Him. Remember, God has the final say. He knows what is best for all of us.

HELL: There are varied reasons why everybody is here and not in heaven. So, I thought about causes and created a small laundry list.

1. They turned their backs on God. They rejected the truth that God does exist or wanted nothing to do with Him, believing spiritual matters were a total waste of their energy and time.

Judgment

2. They refused to acknowledge their sins to Him, or they never asked God to forgive them.
3. They refused to believe the only way into heaven is through faith in Jesus. Instead, they may have counted on their chosen false spiritual leaders and their represented religions to get them into heaven.
4. Some depended exclusively on their good works or moral character.

The tables have quickly turned. God is now judging them. He has a perfect memory. God knows what everyone did and did not do while living on Earth. Everybody is being severely disciplined and punished. The dreadful consequences are never-ending.

HEAVEN: God is always in charge. Nobody ever challenges or tries to judge God.

* * * * *

Will you opt to <u>judge</u> God?
Will you opt <u>not</u> to judge God?

CHAPTER 34

TWO LOCKED DOORS

A friend asked me why I had so many keys on my key chain. I started to laugh because I could not give them a good answer. First, I tried to determine what every key would open, but I was unsuccessful. As a result, I took ¾ of my keys off my chain to lighten the load. But seriously, people only need a few keys, not a boat load.

I thought about the ridiculous number of keys I was carrying around, and God brought the following imagery to mind. Envision two enormous solid wooden doors that are incredibly tall and wide. Both doors have a lock. The keys will either open the door to heaven or hell.

The person in charge asks the first person to give him their key. They gladly hand their key over to him. The key indicates that they are a good person by human standards, maintain high morals, and do more good deeds than bad. They give money to various charities and believe in what their chosen spiritual leader is teaching them.

The person in charge walks over to both doors. The door to heaven remains locked, but the door to hell becomes unlocked. The person is shocked. They are physically grabbed and aggressively shoved through the door.

The second person in line gives the person in charge their key. This key indicates they believe God does not exist, Jesus does not exist, Satan does not exist, demons do not exist, the afterlife does not exist, and the Bible is bogus. Because of their unbelief, the second person does not think their key will open

Two Locked Doors

the door to either hell or heaven. They believe there are other options available.

The person in charge walks over to both doors. The door to heaven remains locked, but the door to hell becomes unlocked. The person in charge shoves the second person through the door head-first.

The last person hands over a key. The key indicates that Jesus does exist. He died an abysmal death on the cross for all of the sins of the entire human race. This person has entrusted their life to Jesus as their Lord and Savior.

The person in charge walks over to the two doors. The door to hell remains locked, but the door to heaven immediately flings wide open.

* * * * *

Will you opt to have your key <u>open</u> the door leading to hell?
Will you opt to have your key <u>open</u> the door leading to heaven?

CHAPTER 35

GOOD AND BAD PEOPLE

People judge the actions and behaviors of other people. Society pigeonholes people as being either good or bad. We might consider them a "good" person if they are kind to others, donate to charities, attend church, and obey the laws. We might think of someone as a "bad" person if they mistreat others, commit crimes, or live solely for pleasure. Everyone makes a personal choice about their actions and behaviors.

<u>**HELL**</u>: Both good and bad people, by human standards, are found here. Does this shock you? Everybody is here because they rebelled and turned their back on God, refused to repent, and chose not to ask for forgiveness of their sins. They said "no" to changing their lifestyle despite God's disapproval. Everyone here is an enemy of God. They made up their rules to follow, devised their plan, and continued to do what they pleased.

<u>**HEAVEN**</u>: Good and bad people, by human standards, are found here. Everybody has repented, asked for forgiveness of all their sins, and tried to change their lifestyle to please God. They acknowledged that because of all of the sins of humanity, Jesus died a horrendous death on the cross. Salvation is a free gift and is available to everyone, regardless of how the world may judge them.

* * * * *

Will you opt to <u>refuse</u> to do what God expects and land in hell?
Will you opt to <u>do</u> what God expects and land in heaven?

* * * * *

Good and Bad People

Some people believe annihilation exists. Annihilation involves complete decimation, elimination, and eradication. The annihilation mindset is everybody who chooses to believe that Jesus paid the sin debts in full will be given eternal life. Everyone else who chooses to reject Jesus will cease to exist once they die. Being severely punished in hell are the people who are non-believers.

HELL: Annihilation is a myth because it is an escape mechanism. The concept ignores the Bible's many references to hell. God has purposely designed hell to be an appalling and upsetting life for everyone who has rejected Him.

HEAVEN: The souls of all believers are spending their eternity with God. He has fulfilled His promise just like He said He would. John 3:36 is just one of many verses that contain this promise: "And anyone who believes in God's Son has eternal life. Anyone who doesn't obey the Son will never experience eternal life but remains under God's angry judgment."

* * * * *

Will you opt to believe people who are promoting the false annihilation theory?
Will you opt to believe the Bible and God that annihilation does not exist?

CHAPTER 36

DIFFERENT ROADS

What is your preference? Do you like to drive on the interstate, roads in a city, town, or the country? Most roads have ample room to drive on while others roads have barely enough room for two cars to pass. The majority of people favor driving on a road with plenty of space over a narrow one.

In Matthew 7:13-14, Jesus taught, "You can enter God's Kingdom only through the narrow gate. The highway to hell is broad, and its gate is wide for the many who choose that way. But the gateway to life is very narrow and the road is difficult, and only a few ever find it." In this illustration, we see that one road is trendy, and the other road is unpopular. The popular road is the <u>broad</u> road. It is flat and smooth, and an easy and unrestricted way to travel. Unfortunately, this road leads straight to hell, and many people will choose it. The other road is the <u>narrow</u> road. This road is bumpy and hilly. It is arduous and challenging, and it has travel restrictions. This road leads straight to heaven. Fewer people will choose this road.

* * * * *

Are you going to choose the <u>broad road</u> leading straight to hell? Are you going to choose the <u>narrow road</u> leading straight to heaven?

* * * * *

The world's population constantly fluctuates as people die and others are born. Today, approximately 7 billion people are living worldwide.

Different Roads

HELL: It is overpopulated. The Bible says <u>the majority</u> of the people will choose the broad road.

75% of 7 billion people = 5.25 billion
95% of 7 billion people = 6.65 billion

Since the beginning of time, there have been approximately 100 billion people who have lived on Earth. Eighty percent of 100 billion people = 80 billion people have chosen the broad road.

HEAVEN: It is underpopulated. The <u>minority</u> of the people will personally choose the narrow road.

25% of 7 billion people = 2.5 billion
05% of 7 billion people = 3.5 million
20% of 100 billion people = <u>20</u> billion people have chosen the narrow road.

* * * * *

Will you opt to end up in an <u>overpopulated</u> hell?
Will you opt to end up in an <u>underpopulated</u> heaven?

* * * * *

Crowds of people are an easy group to follow. I asked myself why people are attracted to a crowd. There are many reasons, but I thought of three things. A group allows people to pretend to be somebody they are not; they will be accepted and not rejected, together with making them think that their sense of security is dependent on a crowd of people. As they say, don't follow the 'masses' because sometimes the 'm' is silent!

Minor or major problems can occur because of a crowd of people. Some crowd followers will question their way of thinking when the crowd does something that they think is objectionable but will accept it. When the followers acquire this wrong mindset, they will quickly choose to change their moral compass to match the moral compass of the crowd.

God, Jesus, Satan, and the demons do not think the same way about all of humanity. God and Jesus love everybody. They view everyone as being special, unique, and valuable. Satan and the demons, on the other hand, loathe everybody. They believe the entire human race is trash, having no value or worth.

God brought to my mind the image of an artist who takes a blank canvas and turns it into a beautiful piece of artwork. Likewise, God views people as His priceless handiwork and unique masterpieces. In Psalm 139:14, David writes, "Thank you for making me so wonderfully complex! Your workmanship is marvelous—how well I know it!" We are His precious and treasured artwork. God, being the best artist ever, loves looking at His majestic work.

God is flawless, genuine, reliable, and trustworthy 100% of the time. He will never leave you high and dry. During the good, hard, and challenging times, God will care for you.

Crowd followers are looking for someone to fill the void in their personal lives. They choose a crowd of people and not God. There are distinct differences between a crowd and God. When a crowd disbands, their acceptance, safety, and belonging will come to an abrupt end. Crowds of people are unreliable 100% of the time because of their deficiencies and flaws. Their connection with people is only temporary and brief. God, on the other hand, never leaves, He is reliable 100% of the time, and His connection with people is forever. Making the correct choice takes courage. When people decide not to

Different Roads

follow the crowd but to follow God exclusively, they make the right choice.

* * * * *

Will you opt to <u>follow the crowd</u> taking the broad road and ending up in hell?
Will you opt to <u>follow God</u> taking the narrow road and ending up in heaven?

CHAPTER 37

SATAN LIES

A friend of mine told me when she was a child, her mother told her not to go to the next-door neighbor's property and eat their raspberries. She did not listen to her mother; instead, she succumbed to the peer pressure of her friends. When she got home, her mother asked her if she had been eating raspberries. She looked her mother straight in the eyes and lied, "no." Unfortunately, her mother knew she was lying because her entire mouth was stained with raspberry juice. She was caught red-handed.

Satan is an enticer because he wants us to disobey God. He might tell us to stop taking God's instructions seriously or that it won't be that bad if we defy them; there is more than one way to get to heaven; God does not even exist; once we die, our bodies and our souls cease to exist; after we die, we will be given other opportunities to live again on Earth; and we have plenty of time to think about religious matters later, but for now, we should do what we want. Not one of his lies is true.

The Bible says in John 8:44, "For you are the children of your father the devil, and you love to do the evil things he does. He was a murderer from the beginning. He has always hated the truth, because there is no truth in him. When he lies, it is consistent with his character; for he is a liar and the father of lies." Stop believing the false lies of Satan. Satan should never be trusted because he is the ultimate charmer, con artist, liar, and schemer. His mission is to deceive many people because this is how he tries to get even with God.

Think of Satan holding an expensive and shiny new fishing rod. Before hooking the people with his brazen lies, he reels them in using different lures and baits. They soon realize they should never have believed him.

God is genuine. He is authentic. God has never told one lie. He speaks the absolute truth at all times. God says to choose heaven because it is the best place and hell is the worst place.

HELL: Satan deliberately tells lies about this place. He tricks people into thinking that hell is not that bad. "Liar, liar, pants on fire" is a fantastic way to describe Satan. Everybody arriving here is aggravated, disappointed, and scared. Being in hell never benefits anybody emotionally, mentally, or physically.

HEAVEN: God loves us so much that He sent His son to die in our place so that we may have eternal life with Him.

* * * * *

Will you opt to <u>trust</u> Satan's lies and end up in hell?
Will you opt to <u>trust God's love</u> and end up in heaven?

CHAPTER 38

LAKE OF FIRE

Many people, one day in the future, will physically be thrown into the appalling and spine-chilling Lake of Fire. There will be no way to avoid it. God has no choice because they rejected Him and turned their backs on Him. Never forget that God is unchangeable, and so are every one of His decisions.

The frightening reality of the future Lake of Fire is not bogus. Remember, when God puts people on the alert regarding future events, they will come to pass in His perfect timing. The future Lake of Fire will surpass trillions of years and never come to an end. No one will ever be released from this dreadful place.

God is authentic and deceives nobody. He is very upfront and refuses to hide any facts. God knows the truth will make all of humanity very fearful and ill at ease, but it needs to be told. His truth should never be rejected but always accepted and fully embraced. God has never lied but tells the utter truth at all times. So, always believe what He says.

The Bible clearly describes the future Lake of Fire. I have listed a few verses. This is what it says regarding this abysmal place.

VERSES

The dead were judged according to what? – Revelation 20:12—I saw the dead, both great and small, standing before God's throne. And the books were opened, including the Book of Life. And the dead were judged according to what they had done, as recorded in the books.

Lake of Fire

People whose names are not found in the Book of Life will be what? – Revelation 20:15 – And anyone whose name was not found recorded in the Book of Life was thrown into the lake of fire.

The beast and the false prophet will be thrown how? How is the fiery lake described? – Revelation 19:20 – And the beast was captured, and with him the false prophet who did mighty miracles on behalf of the beast—miracles that deceived all who had accepted the mark of the beast and who worshiped his statue. Both the beast and his false prophet were thrown alive into the fiery lake of burning sulfur.

Satan, the beast, and false prophet will be thrown where? All three of them will be what day and night? How long will the torment last? – Revelation 20:10 – Then the devil, who had deceived them, was thrown into the fiery lake of burning sulfur, joining the beast and the false prophet. There they will be tormented day and night forever and ever.

Their fate will be where? – Revelation 21:8 – But cowards, unbelievers, the corrupt, murderers, the immoral, those who practice witchcraft, idol worshipers and all liars – their fate is in the fiery lake of burning sulfur. This is the second death.

Always remember, God gives everybody their afterlife choice. Even though it causes God great sadness, He will never interfere with your free will to choose. God will allow your final decision to stand.

We need to heed because God does not want anybody to choose to be thrown into the Lake of Fire. He has forewarned us about what to expect. Everyone will have to personally decide if they will choose to spend <u>trillions and trillions and trillions</u> of years in the Lake of Fire with no end in sight. This decision should never be taken flippantly but very seriously.

* * * * *

Will you opt to be <u>physically thrown</u> into the petrifying Lake of Fire?
Will you opt to <u>never</u> be physically thrown into the petrifying Lake of Fire?

CHAPTER 39

NEW JERUSALEM

One day, God will destroy Earth because it is filled with wickedness and many sins. Once the Earth is destroyed, God will bring a new city out of heaven to the new Earth. In Revelation 21, we read about this new city, which will be called the New Jerusalem. It will be impeccable. Everyone whose names are written in the Book of Life will become permanent residents in the New Jerusalem city.

God and the people whose names are found in the Book of Life will live together. Revelation 21: 3 says, "God's home is now among His people! He will live with them, and they will be His people. God Himself will be with them." He will never hide but will physically be seen by everyone, allowing them to converse with Him.

This is only the tip of the iceberg. Just like in heaven, everybody will be eating, working, discovering and exploring, participating in leisure activities of their choice, talking, smiling, and laughing with people in every ethnic group from all over the world, worshipping and praising God, listening to God's teachings, hearing God sing, playing all types of musical instruments, and so much more.

The size of the New Jerusalem city will be enormous. There will be more than sufficient room for the innumerable people. The city will be amazing, blissful, electrifying, safe, sinless, and colorful. This city will be different from all the cities in the world today. The future city will have a variety of fun and exciting jobs. It will have good entertainment and all types of leisure activities.

In Revelation 21:12-13, the Bible says, "The city wall was broad and high, with twelve gates guarded by twelve angels. And the names of the twelve tribes of Israel were written on the gates. There were three gates on each side—east, north, south, and west." Like a giant square, the city wall's length, width, and height will be equal. In Revelation 21:16, the Bible says, "When he measured it, he found it was a square, as wide as it was long. In fact, its length and width and height were each 1,400 miles" In Revelation 21:21, the Bible says, "The twelve gates were made of pearls—each gate from a single pearl! And the main street was pure gold, as clear as glass."

In Revelation 21:23, the Bible says, "And the city has no need of sun or moon, for the glory of God illuminates the city, and the Lamb is its light."

In Revelation 21:25, the Bible says, "Its gates will never be closed at the end of day because there is no night there." Everyone will safely be able to come and go outside of the city at any time. They will be permitted to seek out, discover, explore, and enjoy all of the unknowns.

The future New Jerusalem city will be a melting pot. There will be people from all over the world. Personality conflicts will be non-existent. Everybody will respect everyone else. Everyone will genuinely like each other and get along beautifully.

Twelve precious stones will be on display. In Revelation 21:19-20, the Bible says, "The wall of the city was built on foundation stones inlaid with twelve precious stones: the first was jasper, the second sapphire, the third agate, the fourth emerald, the fifth onyx, the sixth carnelian, the seventh chrysolite, the eighth beryl, the ninth topaz, the tenth chrysoprase, the eleventh jacinth, the twelfth amethyst."

I want you to take the time to get on social media or find books where you can see the 12 different types of precious stones. Keep in mind, precious stones found on the Earth have defects. However, the precious stones found in the city will be flawless.

The Bible says in Revelation 21:27, "Nothing evil will be allowed to enter, nor anyone who practices shameful idolatry and dishonesty—but only those whose names are written in the Lamb's Book of Life."

I want you to anticipate and get excited about the future New Jerusalem city because it will be beyond your wildest dreams.

* * * * *

Will you opt to <u>never live</u> in the New Jerusalem city surpassing trillions of years?

Will you opt to <u>live</u> in the New Jerusalem city surpassing trillions of years?

CHAPTER 40
PREDICTED FUTURE EVENT

Nobody can predict the future. People who pretend to foretell the future are not genuine but are fakes and imposters. God is the only one who knows what will happen in the future.

The only book that accurately foretells future events is the Bible. It has predicted past events and contains prophecies that will occur in the future. The Bible is 100% accurate and can be trusted implicitly. The Bible clearly says everyone alive and living on the earth, in heaven, and hell will do what? The answer is confession. When people confess, they acknowledge someone or something.

The Bible says in Philippians 2:10, "that at the name of Jesus every knee should bow, in heaven and on Earth and under the Earth." This verse tells us that everyone (the entire human race, heavenly beings, Satan, demons, and the fallen angels) will bow down. Then, the foretold confession day will take place. God has pre-arranged the exact date, and time it will transpire.

HELL: Everyone made an erroneous decision regarding Jesus. They refused to accept Jesus and make Him the Lord and Savior of their life. Their acceptance of Jesus would have kept them out of this atrocious place.

The entire human race has all kinds of lame excuses ready to defend their actions and behaviors. They might say they were too busy, the afterlife did not seem important, or thought they would have more time to sort it all out. They might say that instead of believing in Jesus, they were a devout follower of some other religion or false prophet. Excuses and lack of accountability go hand-in-hand.

Predicted Future Event

I cannot understand why some people flat-out reject Jesus. Why are they choosing not to freely cede to Jesus while there is still time before they die? I know, for a fact, their time will eventually run out, and it will be too late for them to change their minds. Their eternal destiny will be in hell and <u>never</u> heaven.

HEAVEN: Everyone made the right decision regarding Jesus. Everybody is vocalizing their gratefulness to God for allowing them to live here forever and ever.

* * * * *

Will you opt to <u>reject</u> Jesus and end up in hell?
Will you opt to <u>accept</u> Jesus and end up in heaven?

CHAPTER 41
FUTURE RETURN

There will be a day that will cause havoc and out-of-control panic in the future. God does not hide any facts in the Bible; instead, He forewarns what to expect. He talks about the Day of the Lord in the books of Matthew and Mark.

Matthew 24:21-22 says, "For there will be greater anguish than at any time since the world began. And it will never be so great again. Therefore, unless that time of calamity is shortened, not a single person will survive. But it will be shortened for the sake of God's chosen ones."

Mark 13:19-20 says, "For there will be greater anguish in those days than at any time since God created the world. And it will never be so great again. In fact, unless the Lord shortens that time of calamity, not a single person will survive. But for the sake of His chosen ones He has shortened those days."

Pay attention and focus. <u>Beware</u>, the two verses mentioned above are clearly putting every human being on red alert.

* * * * *

Will you opt to <u>be</u> living on the Earth and suffering <u>great</u> anguish?

Will you opt <u>not to</u> live on the Earth and suffer <u>no</u> anguish in heaven?

* * * * *

God is the only one who accurately predicts all the future events that will transpire. All of His predictions are found in the Bible. One prediction is the most important, and that is

Future Return

that Jesus will return to Earth. The Bible talks about this event 1,845 times, and 23 of the 27 New Testament books mention it. Also, Jesus Himself spoke 22 times about His return.

God is the only person who knows the exact date, time, hour, minute, and second when Jesus will return. Everybody will see Jesus' return. Some people living on the Earth will join Jesus in the air. They will be on their way to heaven. Everyone will be euphoric. The other people who are left behind will not be going to heaven. They will continue to live in this broken and tragic world for a certain amount of time. The people will endure severe emotional, mental, and physical suffering.

All of the future occurrences will be distressing and spine-chilling. These will be <u>harrowing future happenings</u>.

The predicted future events are not bogus or made-up; instead, they are the real deal. In the Book of Revelation, God clearly warns people what to expect. This is a dire warning and should not be dismissed. The following is guaranteed to take place in the future.

What things will happen? – Revelation 6:12 – I watched as the Lamb broke the sixth seal, and there was a great earthquake. The sun became as black as dark cloth, and the moon became as red as blood.

What will be restrained? – Revelation 7:1 – Then I saw four angels standing at the four corners of the Earth, holding back the four winds so they did not blow on the Earth or the sea, or even on any tree.

Things will become so bad on the Earth that heaven will be silent for how long? – Revelation 8:1 – When the Lamb broke the seventh seal on the scroll, there was silence throughout heaven for about half an hour. When He opened the seventh seal, there was silence in heaven for about half an hour.

A third of what things will be burned up? – Revelation 8:7 – The first angel blew his trumpet and hail and fire mixed with blood were thrown down to the Earth. One-third of the Earth was set on fire, one-third of the trees were burned up and all the green grass was burned.

What things will come to pass in the sea? – Revelation 8:9 – one-third of all the living things in the sea died, and one-third of all the ships on the sea were destroyed.

Water will become what? – Revelation 8:11 – The name of the star is Bitterness. It made one-third of the waters bitter, and many of the people died from drinking the bitter water.

What will be darkened? – Revelation 8:12 – Then the fourth angel blew his trumpet, and one-third of the sun was struck, and one-third of the moon, and one-third of the stars, and they became dark. And one-third of the day was dark, and also one-third of the night.

What things will be darkened by the smoke? – Revelation 9:2 –When he opened it, smoke poured out as though from a huge furnace, and the sunlight and air turned dark from the smoke.

What is found in the smoke? – Revelation 9:3 – Then locusts came from the smoke and descended on the Earth, and they were given power to sting like scorpions.

People will seriously seek out what? They will not find what? What will flee from the people? – Revelation 9:6 – In those days people will seek death but will not find it. They will long to die, but death will flee from them!

Locusts will harm people for how many months? – Revelation 9:10 – They had tails that stung like scorpions, and for five months they had the power to torment people.

Third of the human race will what? – Revelation 9:15 – Then the four angels who had been prepared for this hour and day and month and year were turned loose to kill one-third of all the people on Earth.

What are the three plagues? – Revelation 9:18 – One-third of all the people on Earth were killed by these three plagues – by the fire and smoke and burning sulfur that came from the mouths of the horses.

Painful what will break out on the people? – Revelation 16:2 – So the first angel left the Temple and poured out his bowl on the Earth, and horrible, malignant sores broke out on everyone who had the mark of the beast and who worshipped his statue.

What will happen to all of the life in the sea? – Revelation 16:3 – Then the second angel poured out his bowl on the sea, and it became like the blood of a corpse. And everything in the sea died.

Rivers and springs will become what? – Revelation 16:4 – Then the third angel poured out his bowl on the rivers and springs of water, and they became blood.

People will be burned by what? – Revelation 16:9 – Everyone was burned by this blast of heat, and they cursed the name of God, who had control over all these plagues. They did not repent of their sins and turn to God and give Him glory.

Why will the people grind their teeth? – Revelation 16:10 – Then the fifth angel poured out his bowl on the throne of the beast, and his kingdom was plunged into darkness. His subjects ground their teeth in anguish.

What will happen to the Euphrates River? – Revelation 16:12 – Then the sixth angel poured out his bowl on the great

Euphrates River, and it dried up so that the kings from the east could march their armies towards the west without hindrance.

What will happen? – Revelation 16:18 – Then the thunder crashed and rolled, and lightning flashed. And a great earthquake struck – the worst since people were placed on Earth.

How many pounds will the hailstones weigh? – Revelation 16:21 – There was a terrible hailstorm, and hailstones weighing as much as seventy-five pounds fell from the sky onto the people below. They cursed God because of the terrible plague of the hailstorm.

No doubt, these future events mentioned above will transpire. Nobody can bring them to an end or put a stop to them. God will be in complete and total control. Remember, forewarned is forearmed.

* * * * *

Will you opt <u>not</u> to go to heaven when Jesus returns?
Will you opt to <u>go</u> to heaven when Jesus returns?

CHAPTER 42
CELEBRATED OR MOURNED

When people die, their death will either be celebrated or mourned. Good and bad destinies in eternity happen because of death. When you die, will people celebrate or mourn your death?

<u>**HELL**</u>: When people die on Earth and their eternal destiny will be in hell, their deaths will be sadly mourned.

Most people want to high-tail it and immediately leave the premises. But, if given a choice, they would ask for a second chance to return to Earth and relive their lives pleasing God.

One day, I thought about being granted the privilege of leaving hell. An oversized vehicle came to mind. It was in deep and thick mud and unable to get out of there. All four wheels kept spinning and spinning, but nothing was happening. The vehicle was stuck and unmovable.

Some people believe that others in hell will only be there for some time. They have the mistaken belief that once a predetermined time has elapsed, they will be released and relocated back to Earth or sent up to heaven. This is a whopper lie from Satan. The absolute truth is this will never happen because they are stuck fast in hell; a cruel but true reality.

<u>**HEAVEN**</u>: The people who are going to heaven, their deaths will be celebrated. They will be completely safe and experience daily joy. Nobody will ever entertain the thought of returning to Earth and living in a broken, sad, and fallen world.

Where is Your Eternal Destiny

People who <u>accepted</u> Jesus and <u>asked</u> for forgiveness of their sins are now in heaven. The other people who <u>rejected</u> Jesus and <u>refused</u> to ask forgiveness for their sins are now in hell.

* * * * *

Will you opt to have your death <u>mourned</u>?
Will you opt to have your death <u>celebrated</u>?

* * * * *

When God convicts people to change their life's wrongs, they are held accountable. When people accept God's conviction and decide to change, they wisely obey God.

God has expectations. He wants everybody to take full responsibility for their sins. Second, God wants everyone to confess their sins to Him and ask for forgiveness. When people confess their sins, they are apologetic for what they have done, said, and thought.

The Bible teaches that everyone is a sinner. The entire human race sins against God and other people knowingly and unknowingly. All of humanity has a common denominator. Nobody ever takes a day off from sin. Some sins can be hidden from others, but they can never be hidden from God. He sees and hears everything.

Every sin can be forgiven because Jesus died an abysmal death on the cross. When someone is forgiven, they are permanently exonerated.

* * * * *

Will you opt <u>never</u> to ask forgiveness of your sins?
Will you opt to <u>ask</u> forgiveness of your sins?

* * * * *

God does not give people what they deserve (hell). He gives people what they <u>do not</u> deserve (heaven). Everybody decides where they want God to send them in the afterlife. This is the most crucial decision because it is permanent and unchangeable.

HELL: Some people say they deserve to go here. One day, I thought about this statement because it puzzled me. I came up with reasons why they would say such a thing. They know their lifestyle is wrong, but they are unwilling to change, getting pleasure from all types of sins they know God does not approve of, or they have knowingly and purposefully mistreated others.

People can avoid going here by changing their wrong mindset to the right mindset, putting forth a sincere effort to change what is wrong in their personal life, asking for forgiveness of all their sins, and accepting Jesus' death on the cross as full payment for every one of their sins, and making Him the Lord and Savior of their life.

HEAVEN: Nobody deserves to go to heaven.

Envision a test. The question posed on the exam is, "How do people get into heaven?" There are multiple-choice answers listed, but you must choose the correct one. The answers to choose from are Jesus, Full Dependency on Yourself, and Rejection of God.

The <u>correct</u> answer is "Jesus" alone plus nothing else. This allows people to enter heaven.

The <u>wrong</u> answer is "Full Dependency on Yourself." Being a "good" person will not get you into heaven. Living a good and clean life, being a courteous, kindhearted, and peaceful person, volunteering to help others and the community, donating money to worthy causes, and doing other good works will not get you into heaven. The bottom line is nobody can earn their way into heaven.

The wrong answer is "Rejecting God." Denying the existence of God, rebelling, and refusing to confess and ask forgiveness of personal sins. These things will cause the entrance into heaven to be forbidden.

* * * * *

Will you opt to <u>flunk</u> the test and go to hell?
Will you opt to <u>pass</u> the test and go to heaven?

* * * * *

Sometimes people will say someone gave up their own life so they could escape a hazardous situation. While living on Earth, Jesus willingly died an excruciating death on the cross to save the entire human race from entering the most dangerous places in hell and the future Lake of Fire.

* * * * *

What does a Lord do?

* * * * *

What is the role of a "Lord?" They have complete power over the people. The Lord controls everyone, but nobody controls the Lord.

Jesus wants to be the Lord of your life. You have to allow Jesus to become your Lord personally. You will have to decide to willingly get out of the driver's seat and hand the keys over to Jesus so He can become the new driver.

CHAPTER 43

THE BIBLE

Some people do not trust the accuracy of the Bible. Some believe it is an allegory rather than the literal Word of God. The Bible talks about God, Jesus, Satan, demons, angels, seraphim, cherubim, false spiritual leaders, and true spiritual leaders. It also teaches about hell and the future Lake of Fire, together with heaven and the future New Jerusalem city. These people believe that these are fictional and not factual.

Always remember that the Bible is 100% accurate. The entire Bible is always spot on. It is never obsolete or behind the times. The Bible is always beneficial to the entire human race. It tells everyone how to live their lives and what to avoid doing during their lifetime. Everyone has questions, and the Bible has all the answers.

Take the time to open the Bible. Next, read and focus on what it is saying. Make the Bible the guidepost for your life. It is the wisest book ever written.

CHAPTER 44

LIFE, DEATH, AND THE AFTERLIFE

One day, I thought about life. I concluded that life on Earth is short-lived. It is not everlasting. When people wake up in the morning, they have the mindset they will be alive for the entire day. People do not realize that just because they wake up in the morning, there is no guarantee they will not die that day. Do not think you have escaped death just because you opened your eyes in the morning. Make the most of every day. Today might be your last day on Earth.

Everybody has a specific time frame allotted to them on Earth. Everyone will eventually die one day, and their life here will come to an abrupt end. God is not subject to time. God has no time frame. He has no ending. God will never die. He is eternal. When something is eternal, it is endless, numberless, and timeless.

The afterlife has no time frame. God created the afterlife to have a beginning but not an ending. Since the afterlife has no time frame, it will surpass trillions of years with no end. Do you realize **one trillion <u>seconds</u> is about 31,688 years,** and **one trillion <u>minutes</u> is roughly 1,901,280 years?** Can you imagine being very much alive in the afterlife (heaven or hell) that will surpass trillions and trillions and trillions of years with no ending in sight?

* * * * *

Will you opt to be <u>overwhelmed</u> in the afterlife for trillions and trillions of years?

Will you opt to be <u>ecstatic</u> in the afterlife for trillions and trillions of years?

* * * * *

<u>HELL</u>: Everyone here is eternally separated from the love and protection of God. Hell is atrocious, dreadful, depressing, horrendous, merciless, terrifying, traumatic, and volatile. Nobody is ever happy, laughing, or smiling. It is causing everyone to feel beaten down, hopeless, and overwhelmed. Also, everybody is forced to come to grips with misery, isolation, and all of the harsh, cruel, and vicious realities found here. Everyone is emotionally, mentally, and physically weak. Everybody is a trapped victim here. Because of their severe daily punishments, people are crying, whimpering, wailing, and screaming. Every day gets worse and worse, and crueler and crueler.

<u>HEAVEN</u>: It is just too wonderful for words. Everyone is thoroughly enjoying all the fabulous things found here. It is a picture-perfect paradise. Mansions, precious stones, and streets of gold are found. God is always in complete control of everybody and everything. People are experiencing exhilaration. Everyone feels contented and fantastic. The people smile, laugh, and chat with their reunited loved ones and friends. Everything in heaven is mind-blowing. There is not one harmful or hurtful thing found in heaven. No evil and challenging days occur because every day becomes better and better, and happier and happier.

* * * * *

How do you feel when confronted with the truth of your sinful nature? Does the truth scare you? Do you accept or reject correction? Do you deny your wrongdoing or commit to changing your behavior? Does the truth really set people free?

I have listed a few verses that might challenge you to think about your life. Please do not run away from the truth. Tell God what you think respectfully. Ask Him to give you wisdom, reveal the truth to you, help you to accept the truth, and to be willing to change regarding the truth. God can handle you being 100% honest with Him. He will never push you away because God desperately wants to help you to discover and accept the truth.

You are stronger than you think. To confront the truth head-on takes courage. I believe in you. Press forward using your courage that will allow you to focus on the scriptures below.

* * * * *

What will <u>not be found</u> in heaven is listed below in the following verses.

- ▶ **People who indulge in what things will not inherit heaven?** – 1st Corinthians 6:9-10 – "Don't you realize that those who do wrong will not inherit the Kingdom of God? Don't fool yourselves. Those who indulge in sexual sin, or who worship idols, or commit adultery, or are male prostitutes, or practice homosexuality, or are thieves, or greedy people, or drunkards, or are abusive, or cheat people—none of these will inherit the Kingdom of God."
- ▶ **People will not go to heaven because of what things?** – Galatians 5:19-21 – "When you follow the desires of your sinful nature, the results are very clear: sexual immorality, impurity, lustful pleasures, idolatry, sorcery, hostility, quarreling, jealousy, outbursts of anger, selfish

Life, Death, and the Afterlife

ambition, dissension, division, envy, drunkenness, wild parties, and other sins like these. Let me tell you again, as I have before, that anyone living that sort of life will not inherit the Kingdom of God."

▶ **People who are what three things will not be found in heaven?** – Ephesians 5:5 – "You can be sure that no immoral, impure, or greedy person will inherit the Kingdom of Christ and of God. For a greedy person is an idolater, worshiping the things of this world."

▶ **People who hate other people are what at heart?** – 1st John 3:15 – "Anyone who hates another brother or sister is really a murderer at heart. And you know that murderers don't have eternal life within them."

* * * * *

When people repent, they acknowledge their wrong doing. Because God loves us so much, He wants us to ask forgiveness, repent, and turn away from our sins. Change requires taking the necessary steps to modify our behavior. Changing wrong things into the right things is a hard thing to do, but it is achievable.

People who repent and are <u>willing</u> to change will have an <u>amazing</u> life in heaven. The people who <u>refuse</u> to repent and change will have a <u>traumatic</u> life in hell.

* * * * *

Will you opt to <u>refuse</u> to repent of your sins and strive to change?
Will you opt to <u>repent</u> of your sins and strive to change?

* * * * *

God makes many promises in the Bible, but He never promises another day. Therefore, you mustn't procrastinate when deciding your eternal destiny. You never know if today will be your last day on Earth.

You should never procrastinate when it comes to the afterlife. I knew people who died unexpectedly for various reasons. Some of their lives were celebrated because they are now in heaven. Other lives were mourned because they are in hell at this very moment. Remember, and never forget, that death comes when you least expect it; therefore, never procrastinate in making the afterlife decision.

* * * * *

The most <u>crucial</u> decision everyone must make is choosing their eternal residency that will last for trillions and trillions of years. It is a personal choice. Everybody needs to be very careful what they decide because their final afterlife decision will become permanent.

If you choose <u>hell</u>, continue to live your life as you please.

If you choose <u>heaven</u>, you need to repent, ask God to forgive all of your sins, and make Jesus the Lord and Savior of your life.

* * * * *

If you want to go to heaven pray the following prayer. You need to mean what you are saying.

"Lord Jesus, I am a sinner. I repent of my sins. I make you my Lord and Savior. Amen."

If you prayed the above-mentioned prayer, immediately find a church in your area that teaches the entire Bible and that Jesus is the only way to heaven.

I hope I will see you in heaven.

CHAPTER 45

VERSES FOUND IN THE BIBLE

New Living Translation

Life

Life and breath of every living thing and every human being is in God's what? – Job 12:10 – For the life of every living thing is in His hand, and the breath of every human being.

There is a time to be what? – Ecclesiastes 3:2 – A time to be born and a time to die. A time to plant and a time to harvest.

Days on the earth

Do not do what? – Proverbs 27:1 – Don't brag about tomorrow, since you don't know what the day will bring.

Nobody knows what? – James 4:14 – How do you know what your life will be like tomorrow? Your life is like the morning fog—it's here a little while, then it's gone.

Days on the Earth are what? – Psalm 39:4 – LORD, remind me how brief my time on Earth will be. Remind me that my days are numbered—how fleeting my life is.

All of our days are what? – Psalm 139:16 – You saw me before I was born. Every day of my life was recorded in your book. Every moment was laid out before a single day had passed.

Days disappear like what? – Psalm 102:3 – For my days disappear like smoke, and my bones burn like red-hot coals.

Days are like what? – Psalm 144:4 – For they are like a breath of air; their days are like a passing shadow.

Days on the Earth are like what? – 1st Chronicles 29:15 – We are here for only a moment, visitors and strangers in the land as our ancestors were before us. Our days on Earth are like a passing shadow, gone so soon without a trace.

My life passes more what than a runner? – Job 9:25 – My life passes more swiftly than a runner. It flees away without a glimpse of happiness.

Life passes as swiftly as the what? – Psalm 102:11 – My life passes as swiftly as the evening shadows. I am withering away like grass.

Fading away like what? – Psalm 109:23 – I am fading like a shadow at dusk; I am brushed off like a locust.

People blossom like a flower and then does what? Like a passing shadow, people will quickly what? – Job 14:2 – We blossom like a flower and then wither. Like a passing shadow, we quickly disappear.

God

Who decides how long we will live? – Job 14:5 – You have decided the length of our lives. You know how many months we will live and we are not given a minute longer.

Death

Everyone will what? – 1st Corinthians 15:22 – Just as everyone dies because we all belong to Adam, everyone who belongs to Christ will be given new life.

Adam's sin brought what? – Romans 5:12 – When Adam sinned, sin entered the world. Adam's sin brought death, so death spread to everyone, for everyone sinned.

Can anyone escape the power of the grave? – Psalm 89:48 – No one can live forever; all will die. No one can escape the power of the grave.

What is precious in the sight of God? – Psalm 116:15 – The Lord cares deeply when His loved ones die.

Some people are what when they die in the Lord? – Revelation 14:13 – And I heard a voice from heaven saying, "Write this down: Blessed are those who die in the Lord from now on. Yes, says the Spirit, they are blessed indeed, for they will rest from their hard work; for their good deeds follow them!"

Dying is what for everyone who is heaven bound? – Philippians 1:21 – For to me, living means living for Christ, and dying is even better.

Some dead people are what than the living? – Ecclesiastes 4:2 – So I concluded that the dead are better off than the living.

What happens to wise and foolish people? – Ecclesiastes 2:16 – For the wise and the foolish both dies. The wise will not be remembered any longer than the fool. In the days to come, both will be forgotten.

What is the same fate for all human beings and animals? – Ecclesiastes 3:19 – For people and animals share the same fate—both breathe and both must die. So people have no real advantage over the animals. How meaningless!

What is better than being born? – Ecclesiastes 7:1 – A good reputation is more valuable than costly perfume and the day you die is better than the day you are born.

After all, everyone does what? – Ecclesiastes 7:2 – Better to spend your time at funerals than at parties. After all, everyone dies—so the living should take this to heart.

Wise people think about what? Foolish people think about what? – Ecclesiastes 7:4 – A wise person thinks a lot about death, while a fool thinks only about having a good time.

No one has the power to prevent what? – Ecclesiastes 8:8 – None of us can hold back our spirit from departing. None of us has the power to prevent the day of our death. There is no escaping that obligation, that dark battle. And in the face of death, wickedness will certainly not rescue the wicked.

People will no longer play a part in what? – Ecclesiastes 9:5-6 – The living at least know they will die, but the dead know nothing. They have no further reward, nor are they remembered. Whatever they did in their lifetime—loving, hating, envying—is all long gone. They no longer play a part in anything here on Earth.

You will look for me, but I will be what? – Job 7:8 – You see me now, but not for long. You will look for me, but I will be gone.

When people die their what is gone? – Job 14:10 – But when people die, their strength is gone. They breathe their last, and then where are they?

All memory of their existence will what? – Job 18:17 – All memory of their existence will fade from the Earth; no one will remember their names.

After people die on the Earth their families will never what? – Job 20:9 – Those who once saw them will see them no more. Their families will never see them again.

Life is dominated by what two things? – Romans 7:24 – Oh, what a miserable person I am! Who will free me from this life that is dominated by sin and death?

People die in a what? – Job 34:20 – In a moment they die. In the middle of the night, they pass away; the mighty are removed without human hand

Like grass, people will soon do what? – Psalm 37:2 – For like grass, they soon fade away. Like spring flowers, they soon wither.

Wicked people will do what once they die? – Psalm 37:10 – Soon the wicked will disappear. Though you look for them, they will be gone.

People are gone like a breath of wind that never does what? – Psalm 78:39 – For he remembered that they were merely mortal, gone like a breath of wind that never returns.

God sweeps people away like what? – Psalm 90:5-6 – You sweep people away like dreams that disappear. They are like grass that springs up in the morning. In the morning it blooms and flourishes, but by evening it is dry and withered.

What blows and people are gone? – Psalm 103:16 – The wind blows and we are gone—as though we had never been here.

Death laid what in my path? – 2nd Samuel 22:6 – The grave wrapped its ropes around me; death laid a trap in my path.

Mankind

The lifetime of everybody is just a what? – Psalm 39:5 – You have made my life no longer than the width of my hand. My entire lifetime is just a moment to you; at best, each of us is but a breath."

People are as worthless as a what? – Psalm 62:9 – Common people are as worthless as a puff of wind, and the powerful are not what they appear to be. If you weigh them on the scales, together they are lighter than a breath of air.

People are like what? – 1st Peter 1:24 – As the Scriptures say, "People are like grass; their beauty is like a flower in the field. The grass withers and the flower fades.

The days of everyone on the Earth is like what? We bloom and what? – Psalm 103:15 -16 – Our days on Earth are like grass;

like wildflowers, we bloom and die. The wind blows over it and it is gone, and its place remembers it no more.

Dust

The dust will return to what? What will return to God? – Ecclesiastes 12:7 – For then the dust will return to the Earth and the spirit will return to God who gave it.

Animals and people came from what and will return to what? – Ecclesiastes 3:20 – Both go to the same place—they came from dust and they return to dust.

God turns people back to what? – Psalm 90:3 – You turn people back to dust, saying, "Return to dust, you mortals!"

Once people die, they return to what? – Psalm 104:29 – But if you turn away from them, they panic. When you take away their breath, they die and turn again to dust.

Bible

All Scripture is what? – 2nd Timothy 3:16 – All Scripture is inspired by God and is useful to teach us what is true and to make us realize what is wrong in our lives. It corrects us when we are wrong and teaches us to do what is right.

Word of God is what? – Hebrews 4:12 – For the word of God is alive and powerful. It is sharper than the sharpest two-edged sword, cutting between soul and spirit, between joint and marrow. It exposes our innermost thoughts and desires.

Why were Scriptures written? – Romans 15:4 – Such things were written in the Scriptures long ago to teach us. And the Scriptures give us hope and encouragement as we wait patiently for God's promises to be fulfilled.

How is the Bible described? – Psalm 119:105 – Your word is a lamp to guide my feet and a light for my path.

The Lord's promises are what? – Psalm 12:6 – The Lord's promises are pure, like silver refined in a furnace, purified seven times over.

We must always do what because the Bible is the absolute truth? – 2nd Corinthians 13:8 – For we cannot oppose the truth, but must always stand for the truth.

Trust

Trust in who? – Proverbs 3:5-6 – Trust in the LORD with all your heart; do not depend on your own understanding. Seek His will in all you do, and He will show you which path to take.

Trust God how long? – Isaiah 26:4 – Trust in the LORD always, for the LORD GOD is the eternal Rock.

Prayers

Who was always praying? – Luke 5:16 – But Jesus often withdrew to the wilderness for prayer.

How long did Jesus pray to God? – Luke 6:12 – One day soon afterward Jesus went up on a mountain to pray, and He prayed to God all night.

Why did Jesus go up into the hills? – Matthew 14:23 – After sending them home, He went up into the hills by Himself to pray. Night fell while He was there alone.

Jesus told His disciples that they should always what? – Luke 18:1 – One day Jesus told His disciples a story to show that they should always pray and never give up.

How are the prayers of a righteous person described? – James 5:16 – Confess your sins to each other and pray for each other so that you may be healed. The earnest prayer of a righteous person has great power and produces wonderful results.

Do what? – 1st Thessalonians 5:17 – Never stop praying.

Pray about what? – Philippians 4:6 – Don't worry about anything; instead, pray about everything. Tell God what you need, and thank Him for all He has done.

Past

Everyone is to do what? – Philippians 3:13 – No, dear brothers and sisters, I have not achieved it, but I focus on this one thing: Forgetting the past and looking forward to what lies ahead.

Existence

God

Who is in heaven? – Psalm 115:3 – Our God is in the heavens, and He does as He wishes.

God made the heavens His what? – Psalm 103:19 – The LORD has made the heavens His throne; from there He rules over everything.

God stoops down and looks on what two things? – Psalm 113:5-6 – Who can be compared with the LORD our God, who is enthroned on high? He stoops to look down on heaven and on earth.

How is God described? – 1st Timothy 1:17 – All honor and glory to God forever and ever! He is the eternal King, the unseen one who never dies; He alone is God. Amen.

Is there more than one God? – Isaiah 45:5 – I am the LORD; there is no other God. I have equipped you for battle, though you don't even know me,

Is there any other God? – Isaiah 45:18 – For the LORD is God, and He created the heavens and earth and put everything in place. He made the world to be lived in, not to be a place of empty chaos. "I am the LORD," He says, "and there is no other.

I am God and there is what? – Isaiah 46:9 – Remember the things I have done in the past. For I alone am God! I am God and there is none like me.

There is no other what? – Isaiah 43:10 – "But you are my witnesses, O Israel!" says the LORD. "You are my servant. You have been chosen to know me, believe in me, and understand that I alone am God. There is no other God—there never has been, and there never will be.

Be still and know what? – Psalm 46:10 – "Be still, and know that I am God! I will be honored by every nation. I will be honored throughout the world."

Imitate who? – Ephesians 5:1-2 – Imitate God, therefore, in everything you do, because you are His dear children. Live a life filled with love, following the example of Christ. He loved us and offered Himself as a sacrifice for us, a pleasing aroma to God.

People who refuse to believe there is no God are what? – Psalm 14:1 – Only fools say in their hearts, "There is no God." They are corrupt and their actions are evil; not one of them does good!

A fool says what in his heart? – Psalm 53:1 – Only fools say in their hearts, "There is no God." They are corrupt, and their actions are evil; not one of them does good!

Jesus

Jesus is what? – Hebrews 13:8 – Jesus Christ is the same yesterday, today, and forever.

Jesus will sit on His glorious what? – Matthew 25:31 – But when the Son of Man comes in His glory, and all the angels with Him, then He will sit upon His glorious throne.

Jesus sat down where? – Mark 16:19 – When the Lord Jesus had finished talking with them, He was taken up into heaven and sat down in the place of honor at God's right hand.

Jesus will be seated where? – Luke 22:69 – But from now on the Son of Man will be seated in the place of power at God's right hand."

Where is Jesus standing? – Acts 7:56 – And he told them, "Look, I see the heavens opened and the Son of Man standing in the place of honor at God's right hand!"

Satan

God is what? He promises to do what on our behalf? – 2nd Thessalonians 3:3 – But the Lord is faithful; He will strengthen you and guard you from the evil one.

Satan wanted to be like the Most what? – Isaiah 14:13-14 – For you said to yourself, 'I will ascend to heaven and set my throne above God's stars. I will preside on the mountain of the gods far away in the north. I will climb to the highest heavens and be like the Most High.'

Satan was immediately thrown out of heaven like what? – Luke 10:18 – "Yes," he told them, "I saw Satan fall from heaven like lightning!

Satan was thrown down to what? – Isaiah 14:12 – How you are fallen from heaven, O shining star, son of the morning! You have been thrown down to the Earth, you who destroyed the nations of the world.

What adorned Satan? – Ezekiel 28:13 – You were in Eden, the garden of God; every precious stone adorned you: carnelian, chrysolite and emerald, topaz, onyx and jasper, lapis lazuli, turquoise and beryl. Your settings and mountings were made of gold; on the day you were created they were prepared.

Heart of Satan became what because of his beauty? – Ezekiel 28:17 – Your heart was filled with pride because of all your beauty. Your wisdom was corrupted by your love of splendor. So I threw you to the ground and exposed you to the curious gaze of kings.

Satan is known as the father of what? – John 8:44 – For you are the children of your father the devil and you love to do the evil things he does. He was a murderer from the beginning. He has always hated the truth, because there is no truth in him. When he lies, it is consistent with his character; for he is a liar and the father of lies.

Some people do not belong to God because they do not do what? – John 8:47 – Anyone who belongs to God listens gladly to the words of God. But you don't listen because you don't belong to God."

Satan does what three things? – John 10:10 – The thief's purpose is to steal and kill and destroy. My purpose is to give them a rich and satisfying life.

Satan prowls around like a what? – 1st Peter 5:8 – Stay alert! Watch out for your great enemy, the devil. He prowls around like a roaring lion, looking for someone to devour.

Satan is what? – Zachariah 3:1 – Then the angel showed me Jeshua the high priest standing before the angel of the LORD. The Accuser, Satan, was there at the angel's right hand, making accusations against Jeshua.

Satan did what to Paul? – 1st Thessalonians 2:18 – We wanted very much to come to you, and I, Paul, tried again and again, but Satan prevented us.

Satan does what to the unbelievers? – 2nd Corinthians 4:4 – Satan, who is the god of this world, has blinded the minds of those who don't believe. They are unable to see the glorious light of the Good News. They don't understand this message about the glory of Christ, who is the exact likeness of God.

How does Satan masquerade himself? – 2nd Corinthians 11:14 – But I am not surprised! Even Satan disguises himself as an angel of light.

Satan was what? – Revelation 12:9 – This great dragon—the ancient serpent called the devil, or Satan, the one deceiving the whole world—was thrown down to the Earth with all his angels.

Who tempted Jesus in the wilderness? – Matthew 4:1 – Then Jesus was led by the Spirit into the wilderness to be tempted there by the devil.

Resist the devil and he will do what? – James 4:7 – So humble yourselves before God. Resist the devil, and he will flee from you.

Demons

What did the demons scream at Jesus? – Matthew 8:29 – They began screaming at Him, "Why are you interfering with us, Son of God? Have you come here to torture us before God's appointed time?"

Were people possessed by demons? – Mark 3:11 – And whenever those possessed by evil spirits caught sight of Him, the spirits would throw them to the ground in front of Him shrieking, "You are the Son of God!"

Do demons exist? – Luke 9:1 – One day Jesus called together His twelve disciples and gave them power and authority to cast out all demons and to heal all diseases.

Who makes the demons shudder? – James 2:19 – You say you have faith, for you believe that there is one God. Good for you! Even the demons believe this, and they tremble in terror.

Angels, Seraphims, and Cherubims

How many voices of the angels were heard? – Revelation 5:11 – Then I looked again and I heard the voices of thousands and millions of angels around the throne and of the living beings and the elders.

Angels are far greater in what? – 2nd Peter 2:11 – But the angels, who are far greater in power and strength, do not dare to bring from the Lord a charge of blasphemy against those supernatural beings.

The angels are mighty ones who do what? – Psalm 103:20 – Praise the Lord, you angels, you mighty ones who carry out His plans, listening for each of His commands.

Angels are only what? – Hebrews 1:14 - Therefore, angels are only servants—spirits sent to care for people who will inherit salvation.

Angel of the Lord is a what? – Psalm 34:7 – For the angel of the LORD is a guard; he surrounds and defends all who fear him.

The angel was assigned to do what? – Exodus 23:20 – See, I am sending an angel before you to protect you on your journey and lead you safely to the place I have prepared for you.

God will do what? – Psalm 91:11 – For He will order His angels to protect you wherever you go.

What did the angel do one night? – Acts 5:19 – But an angel of the Lord came at night, opened the doors of the jail, and brought them out.

God sent an angel to bring what? – Luke 1:19 – Then the angel said, "I am Gabriel! I stand in the very presence of God. It was He who sent me to bring you this good news!"

People ate what? – Psalm 78:25 – They ate the food of angels! God gave them all they could hold.

How are the seraphim described? – Isaiah 6:2 – Attending him were mighty seraphim, each having six wings. With two wings they covered their faces, with two they covered their feet and with two they flew.

Seraphim had what kind of coal? – Isaiah 6:6 – Then one of the seraphim flew to me with a burning coal he had taken from the altar with a pair of tongs.

Cherubim spread their wings over what? – 1st Kings 8:7 – The cherubim spread their wings over the Ark, forming a canopy over the Ark and its carrying poles.

Cherubim will look down on what cover? – Exodus 25:20 – The cherubim will face each other and look down on the atonement cover. With their wings spread above it, they will protect it.

Amazing True Facts Regarding God

Possible
What is impossible for people is what? – Luke 18:27 – He replied, "What is impossible for people is possible with God."

Builder
God built what? – Hebrews 3:4 – For every house has a builder, but the one who built everything is God.

Creation
God holds what all together? – Colossians 1:17 – He existed before anything else and He holds all creation together.

What began when God spoke? – Psalm 33:9 – For when He spoke, the world began! It appeared at His command.

When did God create the heavens and the Earth? – Genesis 1:1-2 – In the beginning God created the heavens and the earth. The earth was formless and empty, and darkness covered the deep waters. And the Spirit of God was hovering over the surface of the waters.

What day was the light created? – Genesis 1:3-5 – Then God said, "Let there be light," and there was light. And God saw that the light was good. Then he separated the light from the darkness. God called the light "day" and the darkness "night." And evening passed and morning came, marking the first day.

What day was the sky created? – Genesis 1:6-8 – Then God said, "Let there be a space between the waters, to separate the waters of the heavens from the waters of the earth." And that is what happened. God made this space to separate the waters of the earth from the waters of the heavens. God called the space "sky." And evening passed and morning came, marking the second day.

What day were the dry land, sea, plants, and trees created? – Genesis 1:9-13 – Then God said, "Let the waters beneath the sky flow together into one place, so dry ground may appear." And that is what happened. God called the dry ground "land" and the waters "seas." And God saw that it was good. Then God said, "Let the land sprout with vegetation—every sort of seed-bearing plant, and trees that grow seed-bearing fruit. These seeds will then produce the kinds of plants and trees from which they came." And that is what happened. The land produced vegetation—all sorts of seed-bearing plants, and trees with seed-bearing fruit. Their seeds produced plants and trees of the same kind. And God saw that it was good. And evening passed and morning came, marking the third day.

What day were the sun, moon, and stars created? – Genesis 1:14-19 – Then God said, "Let lights appear in the sky to separate the day from the night. Let them be signs to mark the seasons, days, and years. Let these lights in the sky shine down on the Earth." And that is what happened. God made two great lights—the larger one to govern the day, and the smaller one to govern the night. He also made the stars. God set these lights in the sky to light the Earth, to govern the day and night, and to separate the light from the darkness. And God saw that it was good. And evening passed and morning came, marking the fourth day.

What day were the creatures who live in the sea and fly in the air created? – Genesis 1:20-23 – Then God said, "Let the waters swarm with fish and other life. Let the skies be filled with birds of every kind." So God created great sea creatures and every living thing that scurries and swarms in the water, and every sort of bird—each producing offspring of the same kind. And God saw that it was good. Then God blessed them, saying, "Be fruitful and multiply. Let the fish fill the seas, and let the birds multiply on the Earth." And evening passed and morning came, marking the fifth day.

What day was the animals that live on the land and humans created – Genesis 1:24- 31 – Then God said, "Let the Earth produce every sort of animal, each producing offspring of the same kind—livestock, small animals that scurry along the ground, and wild animals." And that is what happened. God made all sorts of wild animals, livestock, and small animals, each able to produce offspring of the same kind. And God saw that it was good. Then God said, "Let us make human beings in our image, to be like us. They will reign over the fish in the sea, the birds in the sky, the livestock, all the wild animals on the Earth, and the small animals that scurry along the ground." So God created human beings in His own image. In the image of God He created them; male and female He created them. Then God blessed them and said, "Be fruitful and multiply. Fill the Earth and govern it. Reign over the fish in the sea, the birds in the sky, and all the animals that scurry along the ground." Then God said, "Look! I have given you every seed-bearing plant throughout the Earth and all the fruit trees for your food. And I have given every green plant as food for all the wild animals, the birds in the sky, and the small animals that scurry along the ground—everything that has life." And that is what happened. Then God looked over all he had made, and he saw that it was very good! And evening passed and morning came, marking the sixth day.

What did God do on the seventh day? – Exodus 20:11 – For in six days the LORD made the heavens, the earth, the sea, and everything in them; but on the seventh day He rested. That is why the LORD blessed the Sabbath day and set it apart as holy.

Creator

God is the maker of what? – Psalm 134:3 – May the LORD bless you from Zion, He who is the Maker of heaven and earth.

God made what things? – Psalm 146:6 – He made heaven and earth, the sea, and everything in them. He keeps every promise forever.

What three things belong to God? – Psalm 89:11 – The heavens are yours and the earth is yours; everything in the world is yours—you created it all.

God made what? – Nehemiah 9:6 – You alone are the LORD. You made the skies and the heavens and all the stars. You made the earth and the seas and everything in them. You preserve them all, and the angels of heaven worship you.

God created what? – Colossians 1:16 – for through Him God created everything in the heavenly realms and on earth. He made the things we can see and the things we can't see—such as thrones, kingdoms, rulers, and authorities in the unseen world. Everything was created through Him and for Him.

Earth

What belongs to the creator? – Psalm 24:1 – The earth is the LORD 's, and everything in it. The world and all its people belong to Him.

God set what? – Psalm 74:17 – You set the boundaries of the Earth, and you made both summer and winter.

God formed what? – Psalm 95:5 – The sea belongs to Him, for he made it. His hands formed the dry land, too.

God called the dry ground and waters what? – Genesis 1:10 – God called the dry ground "land" and the waters "seas." and God saw that it was good.

Sea and Waves

God rules over what? – Psalm 89:9 – You rule the oceans. You subdue their storm-tossed waves.

Teeming with life of what? – Psalm 104:25 – Here is the ocean, vast and wide, teeming with life of every kind, both large and small.

God does what to the sea? – Isaiah 51:15 – For I am the LORD your God, who stirs up the sea, causing its waves to roar. My name is the LORD of Heaven's Armies.

What is told to stop here? – Job 38:11 – I said, 'This far and no farther will you come. Here your proud waves must stop!'

Stars

How did God create the starry hosts? – Psalm 33:6 – The LORD merely spoke and the heavens were created. He breathed the word and all the stars were born.

God counts the number of what? He gives all of them what? – Psalm 147:4 – He counts the stars and calls them all by name.

God brings all of the stars out like a what? – Isaiah 40:26 – Look up into the heavens. Who created all the stars? He brings them out like an army, one after another, calling each by its name. Because of His great power and incomparable strength, not a single one is missing.

When God calls out the stars, what happens? – Isaiah 48:13 – It was my hand that laid the foundations of the Earth, my right hand that spread out the heavens above. When I call out the stars, they all appear in order."

Sun and Moon

God created what things? – Psalm 74:16 – Both day and night belong to you; you made the starlight and the sun.

Greater and lesser lights govern what? – Genesis 1:16 – God made two great lights—the larger one to govern the day, and the smaller one to govern the night. He also made the stars.

What does this verse say about the sun? – Psalm 19:6 – The sun rises at one end of the heavens and follows its course to the other end. Nothing can hide from its heat.

Sun and moon will never do what? – Psalm 121:6 – The sun will not harm you by day, nor the moon at night.

Moon and stars were set in what? – Psalm 8:3 – When I look in the night sky and consider the work of your fingers – the moon and the stars you set in place.

Clouds

God causes all of the clouds to do what? – Psalm 135:7 – He causes the clouds to rise over the whole Earth. He sends the lightning with the rain and releases the wind from His storehouses.

Mankind And Animals

Man became a living what? – Genesis 2:7 – Then the LORD God formed the man from the dust of the ground. He breathed the breath of life into the man's nostrils, and the man became a living person.

God created them male and female and called them what? – Genesis 5:1-2 – This is the written account of the descendants of Adam. When God created human beings, He made them to be like himself. He created them male and female and He blessed them and called them "human."

God calls people by their what? – Isaiah 43:1 – But now, O Jacob, listen to the LORD who created you. O Israel, the one who formed you says, "Do not be afraid, for I have ransomed you. I have called you by name; you are mine.

God gives what to every living thing? – Psalm 136:25 – He gives food to every living thing. His faithful love endures forever.

Why do all of the creatures depend on God? – Psalm 104:27 - They all depend on you to give them food as they need it.

God gives the animals what? – Psalm 104:10-11 – You make springs pour water into the ravines, so streams gush down from the mountains. They provide water for all the animals, and the wild donkeys quench their thirst.

What belongs to God? – Psalm 50:10-11 – For all the animals of the forest are mine and I own the cattle on a thousand hills. I know every bird on the mountains and all the animals of the field are mine.

God made what? – Genesis 1:25 – God made all sorts of wild animals, livestock, and small animals, each able to produce offspring of the same kind. And God saw that it was good.

God causes what to happen? – Psalm 104:14 – You cause grass to grow for the livestock and plants for people to use. You allow them to produce food from the Earth -

Attributes

God is what? – Revelation 22:13 – I am the Alpha and the Omega, the First and the Last, the Beginning and the End."

God is what? There is no other what? – Isaiah 44:6 – This is what the LORD says—Israel's King and Redeemer, the LORD of Heaven's Armies: "I am the First and the Last; there is no other God.

I alone am what? – Isaiah 48:12 – Listen to me, O family of Jacob, Israel my chosen one! I alone am God, the First and the Last.

Good and Great

God is what? – 1st Peter 2:3 – now that you have tasted that the Lord is good.

God is what? – Psalm 116:5 – How kind the LORD is! How good he is! So merciful, this God of ours!

Give what because God is good? – Psalm 118:1 – Give thanks to the LORD, for he is good! His faithful love endures forever.

God is good and only does what? – Psalm 119:68 – You are good and do only good; teach me your decrees.

How is God described? – 2nd Samuel 7:22 – How great you are, O Sovereign LORD! There is no one like you. We have never even heard of another God like you!

God is what? – Deuteronomy 7:21 - "No, do not be afraid of those nations, for the LORD your God is among you, and He is a great and awesome God.

Loving, Compassoniate and Merciful

God is what? – 1st John 4:8 – But anyone who does not love does not know God, for God is love.

God's love endures how long? – Psalm 107:1 – Give thanks to the Lord, for He is good! His faithful love endures forever.

How is God described? – Psalm 86:15 – But you, O Lord, are a God of compassion and mercy, slow to get angry and filled with unfailing love and faithfulness.

Strong and Powerful

God is what? – Psalm 24:8 – Who is the King of glory? The LORD, strong and mighty; the LORD, invincible in battle.

Look to God because of His what? – Psalm 105:4 – Search for the LORD and for His strength; continually seek Him.

God will show what two things? – Jeremiah 16:21 – The LORD says, "Now I will show them my power; now I will show them my might. At last, they will know and understand that I am the LORD.

God is all what? – Job 36:22 – Look, God is all-powerful. Who is a teacher like Him?

Power of God is what? – Psalm 147:5 – How great is our Lord! His power is absolute! His understanding is beyond comprehension!

Arm of God is what? – Psalm 89:13 – Powerful is your arm! Strong is your hand! Your right hand is lifted high in glorious strength.

God made what things using His powerful arm? – Jeremiah 32:17 – O Sovereign LORD! You made the heavens and earth by your strong hand and powerful arm. Nothing is too hard for you!

How did God form all of the mountains? – Psalm 65:6 – You formed the mountains by your power and armed yourself with mighty strength.

Wisdom, Understanding and Knowledge

Can any human being match the wisdom, understanding, and knowledge of God? – Proverbs 3:19-20 – By wisdom the LORD laid the earth's foundations, by understanding He set the heavens in place; by His knowledge the watery depths were divided, and the clouds let drop the dew.

How did God stretch out the heavens? – Jeremiah 10:12 – But the LORD made the earth by His power, and He preserves it by His wisdom. With His own understanding He stretched out the heavens.

Understanding

Nobody can do what regarding God's understanding? – Isaiah 40:28 – Have you never heard? Have you never understood? The LORD is the everlasting God, the Creator of all the earth. He never grows weak or weary. No one can measure the depths of His understanding.

Wisdom

What things belongs to God? – Daniel 2:20 – He said, "Praise the name of God forever and ever, for He has all wisdom and power.

Can we understand the wisdom of God? – Romans 11:33 – Oh, how great are God's riches and wisdom and knowledge! How impossible it is for us to understand His decisions and His ways!

God gives the right what? – Proverbs 16:1 – We can make our own plans, but the LORD gives the right answer.

Thoughts and Ways

Are God's thoughts and ways different than the entire human race? – Isaiah 55:8 – "My thoughts are nothing like your thoughts," says the LORD "And my ways are far beyond anything you could imagine.

God's ways and thoughts are what? – Isaiah 55:9 – For just as the heavens are higher than the earth, so my ways are higher than your ways and my thoughts higher than your thoughts.

Plans

God's plans are what? – Jeremiah 29:11 – For I know the plans I have for you," says the LORD. "They are plans for good and not for disaster, to give you a future and a hope.

Prayers

God hears the prayers of the entire human race every day. Does God answer every prayer? – Isaiah 65:24 – I will answer them before they even call to me. While they are still talking about their needs, I will go ahead and answer their prayers!

When we call on God, He promises to do what? – Jeremiah 29:12 – In those days when you pray, I will listen.

God did what two things? – Psalm 66:19 – But God did listen! He paid attention to my prayer.

God's Words

God's words will never what? – Matthew 24:35 – Heaven and earth will disappear, but my words will never disappear.

What will never pass away? – Luke 21:33 – Heaven and earth will disappear, but my words will never disappear.

God's promises prove what? – Psalm 18:30 – God's way is perfect. All the Lord's promises prove true. He is a shield for all who look to Him for protection.

The word of the Lord always holds what? – Psalm 33:4 – For the word of the LORD holds true and we can trust everything He does.

Every what is proven true? – Proverbs 30:5 – Every word of God proves true. He is a shield to all who come to Him for protection.

Do not do what with the words of God? – Proverbs 30:6 – Do not add to His words, or He may rebuke you and expose you as a liar.

Word of God endures how long? – Isaiah 40:8 – The grass withers and the flowers fade, but the word of our God stands forever."

God's word is what? How does it stand in heaven? – Psalm 119:89 – Your eternal word, O LORD, stands firm in heaven.

Truth, Lying, Sinning, and Temptation

What sets people free? – John 8:32 – And you will know the truth and the truth will set you free."

God does not do what? – Titus 1:2 – This truth gives them confidence that they have eternal life, which God—who does not lie—promised them before the world began.

What is impossible? – Hebrew 6:18 – So God has given both His promise and His oath. These two things are unchangeable because it is impossible for God to lie. Therefore, we who have fled to Him for refuge can have great confidence as we hold to the hope that lies before us.

Does God lie or change His mind? – Numbers 23:19 – God is not a man, so He does not lie. He is not human, so He does not change His mind. Has He ever spoken and failed to act? Has He ever promised and not carried it through?

God will not do what? – 1st Samuel 15:29 – And He who is the Glory of Israel will not lie, nor will He change His mind, for He is not human that He should change His mind!"

God does not do what? – Job 34:10 – Listen to me, you who have understanding. Everyone knows that God doesn't sin! The Almighty can do no wrong.

God does not do what? – Deuteronomy 32:4 – He is the Rock; His deeds are perfect. Everything He does is just and fair. He is a faithful God who does no wrong; how just and upright He is!

God is never tempted to do what? Does God tempt any person? – James 1:13 – And remember, when you are being tempted, do not say, "God is tempting me." God is never tempted to do wrong and He never tempts anyone else.

Teacher

God teaches people His what? – Psalm 25:9 – He leads the humble in doing right, teaching them His way.

Does God teach what is best for people? – Isaiah 48:17 – This is what the LORD says—your Redeemer, the Holy One of Israel: "I am the LORD your God, who teaches you what is good for you and leads you along the paths you should follow.

Sings

God does what? – Zephaniah 3:17 – For the LORD your God is living among you. He is a mighty savior. He will take delight in you with gladness. With His love, He will calm all your fears. He will rejoice over you with joyful songs."

God's Timeline

God will live how long? – Hebrews 1:12 – You will fold them up like a cloak and discard them like old clothing. But you are always the same; you will live forever."

A thousand years to God are like what? – Psalm 90:4 – For you, a thousand years are as a passing day, as brief as a few night hours.

One day to God is like how many years? – 2nd Peter 3:8 – But you must not forget this one thing, dear friends: A days is like a thousand years to the Lord, and a thousand years is like a day.

Heaven, Water, Earth, Clouds, and Wind

Heaven

God rides across what? – Psalm 68:33 – Sing to the one who rides across the ancient heavens, His mighty voice thundering from the sky.

Water

What does God do on the waves of the sea? – Job 9:8 – He alone has spread out the heavens and marches on the waves of the sea.

Earth

What does God do on the heights of the earth? – Amos 4:13 – For the LORD is the one who shaped the mountains, stirs up the winds, and reveals His thoughts to mankind. He turns the light of dawn into darkness and treads on the heights of the earth. The LORD God of Heaven's Armies is His name!

Clouds

God makes what His chariot? – Psalm 104:2-4 – You are dressed in a robe of light. You stretch out the starry curtain of the heavens; you lay out the rafters of your home in the rain clouds. You make the clouds your chariot; you ride upon the wings of the wind. The winds are your messengers; flames of fire are your servants.

Wind

God soared on the wings of what? – Psalm 18:10 – Mounted on a mighty angelic being, He flew, soaring on the wings of the wind.

Opening and Closing

What God closes nobody can do what? What God opens nobody can do what? – Revelation 3:7 – Write this letter to the angel of the church in Philadelphia. This is the message from the one who is holy and true, the one who has the key of David. What He opens, no one can close; and what He closes, no one can open:

Warnings, Dreams, and Visions

The wise men were warned in a what? – Matthew 2:12 – When it was time to leave, they returned to their country by another route, for God had warned them in a dream not to return to Herod.

God sent an angel to Joseph and told him what in a dream? – Matthew 2:13 – After the wise men were gone, an angel of the

Lord appeared to Joseph in a dream. "Get up! Flee to Egypt with the child and his mother," the angel said. "Stay there until I tell you to return, because Herod is going to search for the child to kill him."

Did Joseph listen to the warning in his dream? – Matthew 2:22 – But when he learned that the new ruler of Judea was Herod's son Archelaus, he was afraid to go there. Then, after being warned in a dream, he left for the region of Galilee.

God speaks to people using what? – Psalm 89:19 – Long ago you spoke in a vision to your faithful people. You said, "I have raised up a warrior. I have selected him from the common people to be king.

In the last days what things will happen? – Acts 2:17 – In the last days, God says, I will pour out my Spirit upon all people. Your sons and daughters will prophesy. Your young men will see visions, and your old men will dream dreams.

False Spiritual Leaders

Many false spiritual leaders will say they have done what kind of things? – Matthew 7:22-23 – On judgment day many will say to me, 'Lord! Lord! We prophesied in your name and cast out demons in your name and performed many miracles in your name.' But I will reply, 'I never knew you. Get away from me, you who break God's laws.'

How are false spiritual leaders described? – Matthew 23:27 – What sorrow awaits you teachers of religious law and you Pharisees. Hypocrites! For you are like whitewashed tombs—beautiful on the outside but filled on the inside with dead people's bones and all sorts of impurity.

False spiritual leaders are called what? – Matthew 23:33 – Snakes! Sons of vipers! How will you escape the judgment of hell?

Where is Your Eternal Destiny

How many people will be deceived by false spiritual leaders? – Matthew 24:5 – for many will come in my name, claiming, 'I am the Messiah,' and will deceive many.

Many false spiritual leaders are found where? – 1st John 4:1 – Dear friends, do not believe everyone who claims to speak by the Spirit. You must test them to see if the spirit they have comes from God. For there are many false prophets in the world.

What do false spiritual leaders do to people? – Isaiah 9:16 – For the leaders of the people have misled them. They have led them down the path of destruction.

Punishment of False Spiritual Leaders

False spiritual leaders will be sent to the lowest what in hell? – Isaiah 14:15 – Instead, you will be brought down to the place of the dead, down to its lowest depths.

What awaits false spiritual leaders? – Matthew 23:13 – What sorrow awaits you teachers of religious law and you Pharisees. Hypocrites! For you shut the door of the Kingdom of Heaven in people's faces. You won't go in yourselves and you don't let others enter either.

False spiritual leaders will receive what kind of condemnation? – Matthew 23:14 – How terrible it will be for you, scribes and Pharisees, you hypocrites! You devour widows' houses and say long prayers to cover it up. Therefore, you will receive greater condemnation!

False spiritual leaders will be punished how? – Luke 20:46-47 – Beware of these teachers of religious law! For they like to parade around in flowing robes and love to receive respectful greetings as they walk in the marketplaces. and how they love the seats of honor in the synagogues and the head table at banquets. Yet they shamelessly cheat widows out of their property and then pretend to be pious by making long prayers in public. Because of this, they will be severely punished."

Separation from God

People will be shut out from the presence of who? – 2nd Thessalonians 1:9 – They will be punished with everlasting destruction and shut out from the presence of the Lord and from the majesty of His power.

People are what when they do not take refuge in God? – Psalm 34:22 – But the LORD will redeem those who serve Him. No one who takes refuge in Him will be condemned.

God destroys people because they do what to Him? – Psalm 73:27 – Those who desert Him will perish, for you destroy those who abandon you.

Enemies of God

God cannot be what? – Galatians 6:7 – Don't be misled – you cannot mock the justice of God. You will always harvest what you plant.

People who choose to be a friend to the world becomes what? – James 4:4 – You adulterers! Don't you realize that friendship with the world makes you an enemy of God? I say it again: If you want to be a friend of the world, you make yourself an enemy of God.

They told God what? – Job 22:17 – For they said to God, 'Leave us alone! What can the Almighty do to us?'

The people did not want what? – Job 21:14 – And yet they say to God, 'Go away. We want no part of you and your ways.

They love what rather than God? – 2nd Timothy 3:4 – They will betray their friends, be reckless, be puffed up with pride and love pleasure rather than God.

God will do what to all of His enemies? – Psalm 21:8 – You will capture all your enemies. Your strong right hand will seize all who hate you.

Who disappears like smoke? – Psalm 37:20 – But the wicked will die. The LORD's enemies are like flowers in a field—they will disappear like smoke.

God will do what to His enemies? – Isaiah 42:13 – The LORD will march forth like a mighty hero; He will come out like a warrior, full of fury. He will shout His battle cry and crush all His enemies.

God will do what to the heads of His enemies? – Psalm 68:21 – But God will smash the heads of His enemies, crushing the skulls of those who love their guilty ways.

God will erase what from the Earth? – Psalm 34:16 – But the LORD turns His face against those who do evil; He will erase their memory from the Earth.

God does what to His enemies? – Psalm 76:8 – From heaven you sentenced your enemies; the Earth trembled and stood silent before you.

What will happen to God's enemies? – Psalm 92:9 – Your enemies, LORD, will surely perish; all evildoers will be scattered.

Enemies of Jesus

Enemies of Jesus are headed for what? – Philippians 3:18-19 – For I have told you often before and I say it again with tears in my eyes, that there are many whose conduct shows they are really enemies of the cross of Christ. They are headed for destruction. Their god is their appetite, they brag about shameful things and they think only about this life here on Earth.

How many angels could have wiped out all of Jesus' enemies if He had asked for their assistance? – Matthew 26:53 – Don't you realize that I could ask my Father for thousands of angels to protect us and He would send them instantly?

Judas

Judas was remorseful because Jesus had been condemned to what? – Matthew 27:3 – When Judas, who had betrayed Him, realized that Jesus had been condemned to die, he was filled with remorse. So he took the thirty pieces of silver back to the leading priests and the elders.

Judas acknowledged that he betrayed Jesus who was what kind of man? – Matthew 27:4 – "I have sinned," he declared, "for I have betrayed an innocent man." "What do we care?" they retorted. "That's your problem."

What did Judas do because of falsely accusing Jesus? – Matthew 27:5 – Then Judas threw the silver coins down in the Temple and went out and hanged himself.

Arrested

Jesus was what? – Matthew 26:50 – Jesus said, "My friend, go ahead and do what you have come for." Then the others grabbed Jesus and arrested Him.

Jesus was taken to what person? – Matthew 26:57 – Then the people who had arrested Jesus led Him to the home of Caiaphas, the high priest, where the teachers of religious law and the elders had gathered.

Who was looking for evidence against Jesus? – Mark 14:55 – Inside, the leading priests and the entire high council were trying to find evidence against Jesus, so they could put Him to death. But they couldn't find any.

Leading Priests

Who was accusing Him? – Luke 23:10 – Meanwhile, the leading priests and the teachers of religious law stood there shouting their accusations.

Who was trying to find false witnesses who would be willing to lie about Jesus? – Matthew 26:59 – Inside, the leading priests and the entire high council were trying to find witnesses who would lie about Jesus, so they could put Him to death.

Who was making plans for putting Jesus to death? – Matthew 27:1 – Very early in the morning the leading priests and the elders of the people met again to lay plans for putting Jesus to death.

Pilate

After Jesus was arrested, where was He taken? – Matthew 27:2 – Then they bound Him, led Him away and took Him to Pilate, the Roman governor.

Pilate knew the religious leaders had arrested Jesus out of what? – Matthew 27:18 – (He knew very well that the religious leaders had arrested Jesus out of envy.)

Who handed Jesus over to Pilate? – Mark 15:1 – Very early in the morning the leading priests, the elders, and the teachers of religious law—the entire high council—met to discuss their next step. They bound Jesus, led Him away, and took Him to Pilate, the Roman governor.

Jesus' Response

What did the leading priests do to Jesus? – Mark 15:3-5 – Then the leading priests kept accusing Him of many crimes, and Pilate asked Him, "Aren't you going to answer them? What about all these charges they are bringing against you?" But Jesus said nothing, much to Pilate's surprise.

After Jesus heard the false accusations against Him, He remained what? – Matthew 27:12 – But when the leading priests and the elders made their accusations against Him, Jesus remained silent.

Did Jesus respond to any of the false charges against Him? – Matthew 27:14 – But Jesus made no response to any of the charges, much to the governor's surprise.

Released From Prison

During the Passover celebration what would happen? – Matthew 27:15 – Now it was the governor's custom each year during the Passover celebration to release one prisoner to the crowd—anyone they wanted.

Who was a notorious prisoner? – Matthew 27:16 – This year there was a notorious prisoner, a man named Barabbas.

Crowds of people had to decide what? – Matthew 27:17 – As the crowds gathered before Pilate's house that morning, he asked them, "Which one do you want me to release to you— Barabbas, or Jesus who is called the Messiah?"

What people persuaded the crowd to decide to put Jesus to death? – Matthew 27:20 – Meanwhile, the leading priests and the elders persuaded the crowd to ask for Barabbas to be released and for Jesus to be put to death.

Crowd wanted Barabbas to be what? – Matthew 27:21 – So the governor asked again, "Which of these two do you want me to release to you?" The crowd shouted back, "Barabbas!"

The mob shouted what? – Matthew 27:22-23 – Pilate responded, "Then what should I do with Jesus who is called the Messiah?" They shouted back, "Crucify Him!" "Why?" Pilate demanded. "What crime has He committed?" But the mob roared even louder, "Crucify Him!"

Who was going to take responsibility for Jesus' death? – Matthew 27:25 – And all the people yelled back, "We will take responsibility for His death—we and our children!"

People kept shouting what? – Luke 23:21 – But they kept shouting, "Crucify Him! Crucify Him!"

Jesus' Sentence

Jesus was sentenced to what? – Luke 23:24 – So Pilate sentenced Jesus to die as they demanded.

Obedience

Jesus humbled Himself in what? – Philippians 2:8 – He humbled Himself in obedience to God and died a criminal's death on a cross.

Jesus humbled Himself by becoming what? – Philippians 2:6-8 – Though He was God, He did not think of equality with God as something to cling to. Instead, He gave up His divine privileges; He took the humble position of a slave and was born as a human being. When He appeared in human form, He humbled Himself in obedience to God and died a criminal's death on a cross.

Jesus' Pre-Death and Death on the Cross

How is Jesus' appearance described before dying on the cross? – Isaiah 52:14 – But many were amazed when they saw Him. His face was so disfigured He seemed hardly human and from His appearance, one would scarcely know He was a man.

Pilate

What did Pilate do to Jesus? – John 19:15-16 – "Away with him," they yelled. "Away with him! Crucify him!" "What? Crucify your king?" Pilate asked. "We have no king but

Caesar," the leading priests shouted back. Then Pilate turned Jesus over to them to be crucified. So they took Jesus away.

How many soldiers surrounded Jesus? – Mark 15:16 – The soldiers took Jesus into the courtyard of the governor's headquarters (called the Praetorium) and called out the entire regiment.

Flogged

Jesus was what? – John 19:1 – Then Pilate had Jesus flogged with a lead-tipped whip.

Jesus should never have been what because He was innocent? – Deuteronomy 25:2 – If the person in the wrong is sentenced to be flogged, the judge must command him to lie down and be beaten in his presence with the number of lashes appropriate to the crime.

After Jesus was flogged, what happened to Him? – Matthew 27:26 – So Pilate released Barabbas to them. He ordered Jesus flogged with a lead-tipped whip, then turned Him over to the Roman soldiers to be crucified.

Herod

What did Herod and the soldiers do to Jesus? – Luke 23:11 – Then Herod and his soldiers began mocking and ridiculing Jesus. Finally, they put a royal robe on Him and sent Him back to Pilate.

Soldiers

What did the soldiers put on the head of Jesus? – John 19:2 – The soldiers wove a crown of thorns and put it on His head, and they put a purple robe on Him.

What did the soldiers do to Jesus' face? – John 19:3 – "Hail! King of the Jews!" they mocked, as they slapped Him across the face.

Jesus was wearing what on His head? – John 19:5 – Then Jesus came out wearing the crown of thorns and the purple robe. And Pilate said, "Look, here is the man!"

What did the soldiers do to Jesus? – Mark 15:19 – And they struck Him on the head with a reed stick, spit on Him, and dropped to their knees in mock worship.

What did the soldiers do to Jesus? – Mark 15:20 – When they were finally tired of mocking Him, they took off the purple robe and put His own clothes on Him again. Then they led Him away to be crucified.

Cross

Who had to carry Jesus' cross? – Luke 23:26 – As they led Jesus away, a man named Simon, who was from Cyrene, happened to be coming in from the countryside. The soldiers seized him and put the cross on him and made him carry it behind Jesus.

Two other criminals were what? – Luke 23:32 – Two others, both criminals, were led out to be executed with Him.

What did the soldiers do to Jesus? – Luke 23:36 – The soldiers mocked Him, too, by offering Him a drink of sour wine.

Was Jesus innocent unlike the two criminals beside Him? – Luke 23:41 – We deserve to die for our crimes, but this man hasn't done anything wrong."

Darkness fell across the whole land until what time? – Luke 23:44 – By this time it was about noon and darkness fell across the whole land until three o'clock.

What did Jesus call out? – Luke 23:46 – Then Jesus shouted, "Father, I entrust my spirit into your hands!" And with those words He breathed His last.

After Jesus was crucified what did the soldiers do to His clothing? – Matthew 27:35 – After they had nailed Him to the cross, the soldiers gambled for His clothes by throwing dice.

The two criminals were what? – Matthew 27:38 – Two revolutionaries were crucified with Him, one on the right and one on the left.

Jesus was where? – John 19:18 – There they nailed Him to the cross. Two others were crucified with Him, one on either side, with Jesus between them.

The message of the cross is foolish to those who are headed for where? – 1st Corinthians 1:18 – The message of the cross is foolish to those who are headed for destruction! But we who are being saved know it is the very power of God.

Jesus is alive forever and what? Jesus holds the keys of what? – Revelation 1:18 – I am the living one. I died, but look—I am alive forever and ever! And I hold the keys of death and the grave.

Wicked People

There is no what for the wicked? – Isaiah 57:21 – There is no peace for the wicked," says my God.

The joy of the godless has been what? – Job 20:5 – the triumph of the wicked has been short lived and the joy of the godless has been only temporary?

The days of the wicked will never what? – Ecclesiastes 8:13 – The wicked will not prosper, for they do not fear God. Their days will never grow long like the evening shadows.

Years of the wicked are what? – Proverbs 10:27 – Fear of the LORD lengthens one's life, but the years of the wicked are cut short.

Way of the wicked leads to what? – Psalm 1:6 – For the LORD watches over the path of the godly, but the path of the wicked leads to destruction.

Wicked will what in the presence of God? – Psalm 68:2 – Blow them away like smoke. Melt them like wax in a fire. Let the wicked perish in the presence of God.

The wicked are what? – Proverbs 10:25 – When the storms of life come, the wicked are whirled away, but the godly have a lasting foundation.

Expectations, Hope and Future

All expectations of the wicked will come to what? – Proverbs 10:28 – The hopes of the godly result in happiness, but the expectations of the wicked come to nothing

What dies with the wicked? – Proverbs 11:7 – When the wicked die, their hopes die with them, for they rely on their own feeble strength.

Evildoer has no what? – Proverbs 24:19-20 – Don't fret because of evildoers; don't envy the wicked. For evil people have no future; the light of the wicked will be snuffed out.

Do the godless have any hope when they are cut off? – Job 27:8 – For what hope do the godless have when God cuts them off and takes away their life?

People who have accepted Jesus, their hope will not be what? – Proverbs 23:18 – You will be rewarded for this; your hope will not be disappointed.

There will be no what for the wicked? – Psalm 37:38 – But the rebellious will be destroyed; they have no future.

Troubles

Should everyone in the entire world only accept what? – Job 2:10 – But Job replied, "You talk like a foolish woman. Should we accept only good things from the hand of God and never anything bad?" So in all this, Job said nothing wrong.

Life is what? – Job 14:1 – "How frail is humanity! How short is life, how full of trouble!

God causes what to happen to people who love Him? – Romans 8:28 – And we know that God causes everything to work together for the good of those who love God and are called according to His purpose for them.

God is always found in what? – Psalm 46:1 – God is our refuge and strength, always ready to help in times of trouble.

When we deal with small and large troubles in life, what does God promise to do for us? – Isaiah 43:2 – When you go through deep waters, I will be with you. When you go through rivers of difficulty, you will not drown. When you walk through the fire of oppression, you will not be burned up; the flames will not consume you.

David was overwhelmed by his what? – Psalm 55:2 – Please listen and answer me, for I am overwhelmed by my troubles.

When God tests us with all types of troubles, we will come out as what? – Job 23:10 – But He knows where I am going. And when He tests me, I will come out as pure as gold.

God does what? – 2nd Corinthians 1:4 – He comforts us in all our troubles so that we can comfort others. When they are troubled, we will be able to give them the same comfort God has given us.

The present troubles are what? How long will they last? – 2nd Corinthians 4:17-18 – For our present troubles are small and won't last very long. Yet they produce for us a glory that vastly outweighs them and will last forever! So we don't look at the troubles we can see now; rather, we fix our gaze on things that cannot be seen. For the things we see now will soon be gone, but the things we cannot see will last forever.

What will be forgotten? – Job 11:16 – You will forget your misery; it will be like water flowing away.

Trials

God blesses a person that does what? – James 1:12 – God blesses those who patiently endure testing and temptation. Afterward they will receive the crown of life that God has promised to those who love Him.

Consider it joy when you face troubles of what? – James 1:2 – Dear brothers and sisters, when troubles of any kind come your way, consider it an opportunity for great joy.

Worries and Cares

Why should you give all of your cares and worries to God? – 1st Peter 5:7 – Give all your worries and cares to God, for He cares about you.

Do not worry; instead, trust God because He does what? – Psalm 112:6-7 – Such people will not be overcome by evil. Those who are righteous will be long remembered. They do not fear bad news; they confidently trust the LORD to care for them.

Why should you not worry about tomorrow? – Matthew 6:34 – So don't worry about tomorrow, for tomorrow will bring its own worries. Today's trouble is enough for today.

What did Jesus tell His disciples? – Luke 12:22 – Then, turning to His disciples, Jesus said, "That is why I tell you not to worry about everyday life—whether you have enough food to eat or enough clothes to wear.

Desires

Take delight in who? – Psalms 37:4 – Take delight in the LORD, and He will give you your heart's desires.

God knows every what? – Psalm 38:9 – You know what I long for, Lord; you hear my every sigh.

God gives people what kind of desires? – Psalm 21:2 – For you have given him his heart's desire; you have withheld nothing he requested.

God grants what to those who fear Him? – Psalms 145:19 – He grants the desires of those who fear Him; He hears their cries for help and rescues them.

The godly can expect what? – Proverbs 11:23 – The godly can look forward to a reward, while the wicked can expect only judgment.

The hopes of the godly will be what? – Proverbs 10:24 – The fears of the wicked will be fulfilled; the hopes of the godly will be granted.

Abandons or Forgets

God is always what? – Psalm 16:8 – I know the LORD is always with me. I will not be shaken, for He is right beside me.

God will never do what? – Deuteronomy 31:8 – Do not be afraid or discouraged, for the LORD will personally go ahead of you. He will be with you; He will neither fail you nor abandon you."

When people seek God, He will never do what? – Psalm 9:10 – Those who know your name trust in you, for you, O LORD, do not abandon those who search for you.

God will never leave you but will do what? – John 14:18 – No, I will not abandon you as orphans—I will come to you.

God will not abandon me; instead, God will do what? – Psalm 27:10 – Even if my father and mother abandon me, the LORD will hold me close.

Will God forget you? – Isaiah 44:21 – Pay attention, O Jacob, for you are my servant, O Israel. I, the LORD, made you and I will not forget you.

Punishment

It is a terrible thing to what? – Hebrews 10:31 – It is a terrible thing to fall into the hands of the living God.

God's what is powerful? – Psalm 90:11 – Who can comprehend the power of your anger? Your wrath is as awesome as the fear you deserve.

People will be punished with the anger of God if they do what? – Ephesians 5:6 – Don't be fooled by those who try to excuse these sins, for the anger of God will fall on all who disobey Him.

God rebukes people in His what? He terrifies them in His what? – Psalm 2:5 – Then in anger He rebukes them, terrifying them with His fierce fury.

Some people will remain under God's what? – John 3:36 – And anyone who believes in God's Son has eternal life. Anyone who doesn't obey the Son will never experience eternal life but remains under God's angry judgment.

God does not enjoy doing what? – Lamentations 3:33 – For He does not enjoy hurting people or causing them sorrow.

People will not be punished if they do what? – Ecclesiastes 8:5 – Those who obey Him will not be punished. Those who are wise will find a time and a way to do what is right,

Guilty will not go what? – Nahum 1:3 – The Lord is slow to get angry, but His power is great, and He never lets the guilty go unpunished. He displays His power in the whirlwind and the storm. The billowing clouds are the dust beneath His feet.

They will be what? – Psalm 81:15 – Those who hate the Lord would cringe before Him; they would be doomed forever.

Personal Enemies

Never do what? – Proverbs 24:17 – Don't rejoice when your enemies fall; don't be happy when they stumble.

Some people did what three things? – Obadiah 1:12 – You should not have gloated when they exiled your relatives to distant lands. You should not have rejoiced when the people of Judah suffered such misfortune. You should not have spoken arrogantly in that terrible time of trouble.

Give enemies what two things? – Proverbs 25:21 – If your enemies are hungry, give them food to eat. If they are thirsty, give them water to drink.

Giving an enemy food and water causes what to happen? – Proverbs 25:22 – You will heap burning coals of shame on their heads and the LORD will reward you.

Love who? – Luke 6:27 – But to you who are willing to listen, I say, love your enemies! Do good to those who hate you.

Do what two things? – Luke 6:28 – Bless those who curse you. Pray for those who hurt you.

Judge

Who is the judge? – Psalm 50:6 – Then let the heavens proclaim His justice, for God Himself will be the judge.

Who alone judges? – Psalm 75:7 – It is God alone who judges; He decides who will rise and who will fall.

God is what kind of judge? – Psalm 7:11 – God is an honest judge. He is angry with the wicked every day.

God is able to do what? – James 4:12 – God alone, who gave the law, is the Judge. He alone has the power to save or to destroy. So what right do you have to judge your neighbor?

God will judge people for what? – Ecclesiastes 12:14 – God will judge us for everything we do, including every secret thing, whether good or bad.

God will judge our what? – 1st Samuel 2:3 – Stop acting so proud and haughty! Don't speak with such arrogance! For the LORD is a God who knows what you have done; He will judge your actions.

God will give what? – Psalm 94:2 – Arise, O Judge of the Earth. Give the proud what they deserve.

Judgment Seat

After death what happens? – Hebrews 9:27 – And just as each person is destined to die once and after that comes judgment,

How many people will stand before God's judgement seat? – Romans 14:10 – So why do you condemn another believer? Why do you look down on another believer? Remember, we will all stand before the judgment seat of God.

What will every person receive when they appear before Jesus to be judged? – 2nd Corinthians 5:10 – For we must all stand before Christ to be judged. We will each receive whatever we deserve for the good or evil we have done in this earthly body.

What will not help people on judgment day? – Proverbs 11:4 – Riches won't help on the day of judgment, but right living can save you from death.

Angels are being held until what day? – 2ND Peter 2:4 – For God did not spare even the angels who sinned. He threw them into hell, in gloomy pits of darkness, where they are being held until the day of judgment.

God has kept every angel securely what? – Jude 1:6 – And I remind you of the angels who did not stay within the limits of authority God gave them but left the place where they belonged. God has kept them securely chained in prisons of darkness, waiting for the great day of judgment.

Judging other People

When you judge people and do the same things, you will not escape God's what? – Romans 2:3 – Since you judge others for doing these things, why do you think you can avoid God's judgment when you do the same things?

Do not do what? – Matthew 7:1 – Do not judge others and you will not be judged.

How will we be judged? – Matthew 7:2 – For you will be treated as you treat others. The standard you use in judging is the standard by which you will be judged.

Judgmental people are what? – Matthew 7:3-5 – And why worry about a speck in your friend's eye when you have a log in your own? How can you think of saying to your friend, 'Let me help you get rid of that speck in your eye,' when you can't see past the log in your own eye? Hypocrite! First get rid of the log in your own eye; then you will see well enough to deal with the speck in your friend's eye.

People judges others by what? God looks at what? – 1st Samuel 16:7 – But the LORD said to Samuel, "Don't judge by his appearance or height, for I have rejected him. The LORD doesn't see things the way you see them. People judge by outward appearance, but the LORD looks at the heart."

People needs to look beneath what? – John 7:24 – Look beneath the surface so you can judge correctly.

Forgiving Others

God forgives us, so we must do what? – Colossians 3:13 – Make allowance for each other's faults and forgive anyone who offends you. Remember, the Lord forgave you, so you must forgive others.

God will forgive your sins if you do what? – Matthew 6:14 – If you forgive those who sin against you, your heavenly Father will forgive you.

When you hold things against anybody, you need to do what? – Mark 11:25 – But when you are praying, first forgive anyone you are holding a grudge against, so that your Father in heaven will forgive your sins, too."

If you forgive others, you will be what? – Luke 6:37 – "Do not judge others, and you will not be judged. Do not condemn others, or it will all come back against you. Forgive others, and you will be forgiven.

While Jesus was on the cross, He asked God to do what? – Luke 23:33-34 – When they came to a place called The Skull, they nailed Him to the cross. And the criminals were also crucified—one on His right and one on His left. Jesus said, "Father, forgive them, for they don't know what they are doing." And the soldiers gambled for His clothes by throwing dice.

Stephen asked God to do what? – Acts 7:59-60 – As they stoned him, Stephen prayed, "Lord Jesus, receive my spirit." He fell to his knees, shouting, "Lord, don't charge them with this sin!" And with that, he died.

Golden Rule

Do to others as you would what? – Luke 6:31 – Do to others as you would like them to do to you.

Opposite of Revenge and Avenge

Do what? Avoid what? – Romans 12:14 - Bless those who persecute you. Don't curse them; pray that God will bless them.

What will reward you? What will destroy you? – Proverbs 11:17 – Your kindness will reward you, but your cruelty will destroy you.

Do not get tired of doing what? – Galatians 6:9 – So let's not get tired of doing what is good. At just the right time we will reap a harvest of blessing if we don't give up.

Do not withhold what? – Proverbs 3:27 – Do not withhold good from those who deserve it when it's in your power to help them.

How is everyone to clothe themselves? – Colossians 3:12 – Since God chose you to be the holy people He loves, you must clothe yourselves with tenderhearted mercy, kindness, humility, gentleness, and patience.

The fruit of the Spirt is what? – Galatians 5:22-23 – But the Holy Spirit produces this kind of fruit in our lives: love, joy, peace, patience, kindness, goodness, faithfulness, gentleness and self-control. There is no law against these things!

Revenge

Never take what? – Romans 12:19 – Dear friends, never take revenge. Leave that to the righteous anger of God. For the Scriptures say, "I will take revenge; I will pay them back," says the LORD.

God will take what? – Deuteronomy 32:35 – I will take revenge; I will pay them back. In due time their feet will slip. Their day of disaster will arrive, and their destiny will overtake them.'

God will take what? – Hebrews 10:30 – For we know the one who said, "I will take revenge. I will pay them back." He also said, "The Lord will judge His own people."

God will do what to His enemies? – Deuteronomy 32:43 – Rejoice with Him, you heavens, and let all of God's angels worship Him. Rejoice with His people, you Gentiles, and let all the angels be strengthened in Him. For He will avenge the blood of His children; He will take revenge against His enemies. He will repay those who hate Him and cleanse His people's land."

Do not seek what? – Leviticus 19:18 – Do not seek revenge or bear a grudge against a fellow Israelite, but love your neighbor as yourself. I am the LORD.

What will never leave your house? – Proverbs 17:13 – If you repay good with evil, evil will never leave your house.

Do not pay back anyone with what? – Romans 12:17-18 - Never pay back evil with more evil. Do things in such a way that everyone can see you are honorable. Do all that you can to live in peace with everyone.

Never pay back what? – 1st Thessalonians 5:15 – See that no one pays back evil for evil, but always try to do good to each other and to all people.

Do not do what? – 1st Peter 3:9 – Don't repay evil for evil. Don't retaliate with insults when people insult you. Instead, pay them back with a blessing. That is what God has called you to do, and He will grant you His blessing.

If you do what is wrong what will happen to you? – Colossians 3:25 – But if you do what is wrong, you will be paid back for the wrong you have done. For God has no favorites.

Never say what? – Proverbs 24:29 – And don't say, "Now I can pay them back for what they've done to me! I'll get even with them!"

Avenge

Wait for who? – Proverbs 20:22 – Don't say, "I will get even for this wrong." Wait for the LORD to handle the matter.

God will do what? – Exodus 14:14 – The LORD Himself will fight for you. Just stay calm."

God does what? – 2nd Samuel 22:48 – He is the God who pays back those who harm me; He brings down the nations under me

What will God do? – Jeremiah 51:36 – This is what the LORD says to Jerusalem: "I will be your lawyer to plead your case, and I will avenge you. I will dry up her river, as well as her springs,

God will repay them in what? – Isaiah 65:6 – Look, my decree is written out in front of me: I will not stand silent; I will repay them in full! Yes, I will repay them—

God will do what? – 2nd Thessalonians 1:6 – In His justice He will pay back those who persecute you.

Vengeance

How is God described? – Psalm 94:1 – O LORD, the God of vengeance, O God of vengeance, let your glorious justice shine forth!

God will take vengeance because people refuse to do what? – Micah 5:15 – I will pour out my vengeance on all the nations that refuse to obey me."

Vindicate

God will do what? – Psalm 135:14 – For the Lord will give justice to His people and have compassion on His servants.

The person wants God to do what on their behalf? – Psalm 43:1 – Declare me innocent, O God! Defend me against these ungodly people. Rescue me from these unjust liars.

How does God vindicate? – Psalm 35:24 – Declare me not guilty, O LORD my God, for you give justice. Don't let my enemies laugh about me in my troubles.

Fear Who

People needs to fear who? – Luke 12:4-5 – Dear friends, don't be afraid of those who want to kill your body; they cannot do any more to you after that. But I'll tell you whom to fear. Fear God, who has the power to kill you and then throw you into hell. Yes, He's the one to fear.

God can destroy what two things? – Matthew 10:28 – Don't be afraid of those who want to kill your body; they cannot touch your soul. Fear only God, who can destroy both soul and body in hell.

What can we say with confidence? – Hebrews 13:6 – So we can say with confidence, "The LORD is my helper, so I will have no fear. What can mere people do to me?"

Do not be afraid of mere what? – Isaiah 51:12 – I, yes I, am the one who comforts you. So why are you afraid of mere humans, who wither like the grass and disappear?

Instead of fear, God wants you to be what two things? – 1st Corinthians 16:13 – Be on guard. Stand firm in the faith. Be courageous. Be strong.

Accountability

The wicked think what? – Psalm 10:4 – The wicked are too proud to seek God. They seem to think that God is dead.

People thinks God will never call us to do what? – Psalm 10:13 – Why do the wicked get away with despising God? They think, "God will never call us to account."

People will give what for how they lived their life? – Romans 14:12 – Yes, each of us will give a personal account to God.

Everything is what? We are accountable to whom? – Hebrews 4:13 – Nothing in all creation is hidden from God. Everything is naked and exposed before His eyes, and He is the one to whom we are accountable.

How many idle words will people have to give an account? – Matthew 12:36 – and I tell you this, you must give an account on judgment day for every idle word you speak.

Words will do what? – Matthew 12:37 – The words you say will either acquit you or condemn you.

Hiding and not Watching

Can anyone hide in a secret place from God? – Jeremiah 23:24 – Can anyone hide from me in a secret place? Am I not everywhere in all the heavens and earth?" says the LORD.

There is no hiding from God in darkness because darkness of the night shines as what? – Psalm 139:11-12 – I could ask the darkness to hide me and the light around me to become night—but even in darkness I cannot hide from you. To you the night shines as bright as day. Darkness and light are the same to you.

Can anybody hide from God? – Job 34:22 – No darkness is thick enough to hide the wicked from His eyes.

Some people think that God never does what? – Psalm 10:11 – The wicked think, "God isn't watching us! He has closed His eyes and won't even see what we do!"

Some people believe that God is not doing what? – Psalm 94:7 – "The LORD isn't looking," they say, "and besides, the God of Israel doesn't care."

Afterlife

People are conscious because He is the God of the living and not what? – Mark 12:27 – So He is the God of the living, not the dead. You have made a serious error.

Bowing

Every knee will what? – Isaiah 45:23 – I have sworn by my own name; I have spoken the truth, and I will never go back on my word: Every knee will bend to me, and every tongue will declare allegiance to me"

How many knees are going to bow? – Romans 14:11 - For the Scriptures say, "'As surely as I live,' says the LORD, 'every knee will bend to me, and every tongue will declare allegiance to God."

Every knee will bow in what three locations? – Philippians 2:10 – that at the name of Jesus every knee should bow, in heaven and on Earth and under the Earth,

Choosing Hell or Heaven

God is setting what before everyone? – Jeremiah 21:8 – Tell all the people, 'This is what the LORD says: Take your choice of life or death!

People will receive what two things? – Daniel 12:2 – Many of those whose bodies lie dead and buried will rise up, some to everlasting life and some to shame and everlasting disgrace.

Some people will go away into what? Other people will go away into what? – Matthew 25:46 – And they will go away into eternal punishment, but the righteous will go into eternal life.

Who chooses the right road and who chooses the wrong road? – Ecclesiastes 10:2 – A wise person chooses the right road; a fool takes the wrong one.

Broad road leads where? Narrow road leads where? – Matthew 7:13-14 – You can enter God's Kingdom only through the narrow gate. The highway to hell is broad, and its gate is wide for the many who choose that way. But the gateway to life is very narrow and the road is difficult, and only a few ever find it.

How many people will try to enter through the narrow door into heaven unsuccessfully? – Luke 13:24 – Work hard to enter the narrow door to God's Kingdom, for many will try to enter but will fail.

Will some people be denied heaven and end up in hell? – Matthew 7:21-23 – Not everyone who calls out to me, 'Lord! Lord!' will enter the Kingdom of Heaven. Only those who actually do the will of my Father in heaven will enter. On judgment day many will say to me, 'Lord! Lord! We prophesied in your name and cast out demons in your name and performed many miracles in your name.' But I will reply, 'I never knew you. Get away from me, you who break God's laws.'

Gates

Gates of what? – Job 38:17 – Do you know where the gates of death are located? Have you seen the gates of utter gloom?

Are there gates in heaven? – Psalm 118:19 – Open for me the gates where the righteous enter and I will go in and thank the LORD.

Who is going to enter the gates? – Psalm 118:20 – These gates lead to the presence of the LORD and the godly enter there.

Spins and Ransom

God

God will bring some people to what kind of end? – Ezekiel 26:21 – I will bring you to a terrible end, and you will exist no more. You will be looked for, but you will never again be found. I, the Sovereign LORD, have spoken!"

Jesus

Matthew 5:29-30 – So if your eye—even your good eye—causes you to lust, gouge it out and throw it away. It is better for you to lose one part of your body than for your whole body to be thrown into hell. And if your hand—even your stronger hand—causes you to sin, cut it off and throw it away. It is better for you to lose one part of your body than for your whole body to be thrown into hell.

Mark 9:43 – If your hand causes you to sin, cut it off. It's better to enter eternal life with only one hand than to go into the unquenchable fires of hell with two hands.

Mark 9:45 – If your foot causes you to sin, cut it off. It's better to enter eternal life with only one foot than to be thrown into hell with two feet.

Mark 9:47 – And if your eye causes you to sin, gouge it out. It's better to enter the Kingdom of God with only one eye than to have two eyes and be thrown into hell.

Ransom

Can anybody redeem themselves from death by paying a ransom to God? – Psalm 49:7-9 – Yet they cannot redeem themselves from death by paying a ransom to God. Redemption does not come so easily, for no one can ever pay enough to live forever and never see the grave.

Jesus gave His life as a what for many? – Matthew 20:28 – For even the Son of Man came not to be served but to serve others and to give His life as a ransom for many.

Hell

People in hell will never what? – Job 7:9-10 – Just as a cloud dissipates and vanishes, those who die will not come back. They are gone forever from their home—never to be seen again.

What awaits people who are hell-bound? – Isaiah 24:17 – Terror and traps and snares will be your lot, you people of the Earth.

What was not worth it? – Job 33:27 – He will declare to his friend, "I sinned and twisted the truth, but it was not worth it."

Who did the people reject? – Job 18:21 – They will say, 'This was the home of a wicked person, the place of one who rejected God.'"

I will send you where? – Ezekiel 26:20 – I will send you to the pit to join those who descended there long ago. Your city will lie in ruins, buried beneath the Earth, like those in the pit who have entered the world of the dead. You will have no place of respect here in the land of the living.

Descended as outcasts to what below? – Ezekiel 32:24 – Elam lies there surrounded by the graves of all its hordes, those who were slaughtered by the sword. They struck terror in the hearts of people everywhere, but now they have descended as outcasts to the world below. Now they lie in the pit and share the shame of those who have gone before them.

Does anybody remember God? – Psalm 6:5 – For the dead do not remember you. Who can praise you from the grave?

Who will be swallowed up? – Isaiah 5:14 – The grave is licking its lips in anticipation, opening its mouth wide. The great and the lowly and all the drunken mob will be swallowed up.

Maggots and Worms

What is your sheet? What is your blanket? – Isaiah 14:11 – Your might and power were buried with you. The sound of the harp in your palace has ceased. Now maggots are your sheet and worms your blanket.

Maggots find the people what to eat? – Job 24:20 – Their own mothers will forget them. Maggots will find them sweet to eat. No one will remember them. Wicked people are broken like a tree in the storm.

Will the maggots ever die? – Mark 9:48 – where the maggots never die and the fire never goes out.

Fire

God is what kind of fire? – Hebrews 12:29 – For our God is a devouring fire.

How is the fire described? – Matthew 3:12 – He is ready to separate the chaff from the wheat with his winnowing fork. Then He will clean up the threshing area, gathering the wheat into his barn but burning the chaff with never-ending fire.

The eternal fire is prepared for whom? – Matthew 25:41 – Then the King will turn to those on the left and say, 'Away with you, you cursed ones, into the eternal fire prepared for the devil and his demons.

Pyre is piled high with what? The breath of God does what? – Isaiah 30:33 – Topheth—the place of burning—has long been ready for the Assyrian king; the pyre is piled high with wood. The breath of the Lord, like fire from a volcano, will set it ablaze.

How is the fire described? – Isaiah 33:14 – The sinners in Jerusalem shake with fear. Terror seizes the godless. "Who can live with this devouring fire?" they cry. "Who can survive this all-consuming fire?"

Pit

People go down where? – Proverbs 1:12 – Let's swallow them alive, like the grave; let's swallow them whole, like those who go down to the pit of death.

How is the pit described? – Revelation 20:1 – Then I saw an angel coming down from heaven with the key to the bottomless pit and a heavy chain in his hand.

Angel will throw Satan into the bottomless what? – Revelation 20:3 – The angel threw him into the bottomless pit, which he then shut and locked so Satan could not deceive the nations anymore until the thousand years were finished. Afterward he must be released for a little while.

Coals and Sulfur

What will be rained down? – Psalm 11:6 – He will rain down blazing coals and burning sulfur on the wicked, punishing them with scorching winds.

People will be tormented with what? – Revelation 14:10 – must drink the wine of God's anger. It has been poured full strength into God's cup of wrath. And they will be tormented with fire and burning sulfur in the presence of the holy angels and the Lamb.

What will fall down on the heads of people? – Psalm 140:10 – Let burning coals fall down on their heads. Let them be thrown into the fire or into watery pits from which they can't escape.

Darkness

People will disappear in what? – 1st Samuel 2:9 – He will protect His faithful ones, but the wicked will disappear in darkness. No one will succeed by strength alone.

After people die, they will never see the light of what? – Psalm 49:19 – But they will die like all before them and never again see the light of day.

How are the depths described? – Psalm 88:6 – You have thrown me into the lowest pit, into the darkest depths.

How is the land described? – Job 10:21-22 – before I leave—never to return—for the land of darkness and utter gloom. It is a land as dark as midnight, a land of gloom and confusion, where even the light is dark as midnight.

People are driven from light into what? – Job 18:18 – They will be thrust from light into darkness, driven from the world.

How is the morning described? – Job 24:17 – The black night is their morning. They ally themselves with the terrors of the darkness.

People are doomed to what kind of darkness? – 2nd Peter 2:17 – These people are as useless as dried-up springs or as mist blown away by the wind. They are doomed to blackest darkness.

Destruction

Place of what is uncovered? – Job 26:6 – The underworld is naked in God's presence. The place of destruction is uncovered.

People will slide over the cliff to what? – Psalm 73:18 – Truly, you put them on a slippery path and send them sliding over the cliff to destruction.

People are headed for what? – Philippians 3:19 – They are headed for destruction. Their god is their appetite, they brag about shameful things and they think only about this life here on Earth.

What always follows the people? – Romans 3:16 – Destruction and misery always follow them.

Gnashing Teeth and Weeping

People will be thrown into the fiery furnace, where there will be what? – Matthew 13:42 – And the angels will throw them into the fiery furnace, where there will be weeping and gnashing of teeth.

There will be gnashing of what? – Matthew 24:50-51 – The master will return unannounced and unexpected, and he will cut the servant to pieces and assign him a place with the hypocrites. In that place there will be weeping and gnashing of teeth.

There will be what? – Luke 13:28 – There will be weeping and gnashing of teeth, for you will see Abraham, Isaac, Jacob, and all the prophets in the Kingdom of God, but you will be thrown out.

People will grind their teeth in what? – Psalm 112:10 – The wicked will see this and be infuriated. They will grind their teeth in anger; they will slink away, their hopes thwarted.

Terrors

What grips the people? – Psalm 14:5 – Terror will grip them, for God is with those who obey Him.

When terror comes, people will seek what? – Ezekiel 7:25 – Terror and trembling will overcome my people. They will look for peace but not find it.

What awaits people who turn their backs on God? – Jeremiah 48:43 – "Terror and traps and snares will be your lot, O Moab," says the LORD.

The terror of death does what? – Psalm 55:4-5 – My heart pounds in my chest. The terror of death assaults me. Fear and trembling overwhelm me and I can't stop shaking.

People are swept away by what? – Psalm 73:19 – In an instant they are destroyed, completely swept away by terrors.

Your terrors have done what to me? – Psalm 88:16 – Your fierce anger has overwhelmed me. Your terrors have paralyzed me.

What overtook me? – Psalm 116:3 – Death wrapped its ropes around me; the terrors of the grave overtook me. I saw only trouble and sorrow.

Trapped

People are what? – Lamentations 3:47 – We are filled with fear, for we are trapped, devastated and ruined.

Weakness

People are what? – Isaiah 14:10 – With one voice they all cry out, 'Now you are as weak as we are!

Like a strong man with no what? – Psalm 88:4 – I am as good as dead, like a strong man with no strength left.

Non-Existent

What does not exist? – Ecclesiastics 9:10 – Whatever you do, do well. For when you go to the grave, there will be no work or planning or knowledge or wisdom.

Book of Life

Will any names be erased from the Book of Life? – Revelation 3:5 – All who are victorious will be clothed in white. I will never erase their names from the Book of Life, but I will announce before my Father and His angels that they are mine.

Heaven

Heaven will never be what? – Daniel 2:44 – During the reigns of those kings, the God of heaven will set up a kingdom that will never be destroyed or conquered. It will crush all these kingdoms into nothingness and it will stand forever.

Heaven is what? – Hebrews 12:28 – Since we are receiving a Kingdom that is unshakable, let us be thankful and please God by worshiping Him with holy fear and awe.

Heaven will never be what? – Daniel 7:14 – He was given authority, honor, and sovereignty over all the nations of the world, so that people of every race and nation and language would obey Him. His rule is eternal—it will never end. His kingdom will never be destroyed.

God will give you what? – 2nd Peter 1:11 – Then God will give you a grand entrance into the eternal Kingdom of our Lord and Savior Jesus Christ.

God's home is among His what? – Revelation 21:3 – I heard a loud shout from the throne, saying, "Look, God's home is now among His people! He will live with them and they will be His people. God Himself will be with them.

Crowd of people could not be what? The people will come from every what? – Revelation 7:9 - After this I saw a vast crowd, too great to count, from every nation and tribe and people and language, standing in front of the throne and before the Lamb. They were clothed in white robes and held palm branches in their hands.

People are what in heaven? – Philippians 3:20 – But we are citizens of heaven, where the Lord Jesus Christ lives. And we are eagerly waiting for Him to return as our Savior.

Everyone will be what? – Psalm 84:4 – What joy for those who can live in your house, always singing your praises.

God endows people with what kind of blessings? – Psalm 21:6 – You have endowed him with eternal blessings and given him the joy of your presence.

People are filled with what in God's presence? – Psalm 16:11 – You will show me the way of life, granting me the joy of your presence and the pleasures of living with you forever.

God delights in His what? – Psalm 149:4 – For the LORD delights in His people; He crowns the humble with victory.

What kind of treasure are the children of God? – Malachi 3:17 – "They will be my people," says the Lord of Heaven's Armies. "On the day when I act in judgment, they will be my own special treasure. I will spare them as a father spares an obedient child."

People will never be what again in heaven? – Revelation 7:16 – They will never again be hungry or thirsty; they will never be scorched by the heat of the sun.

No human mind can what? – 1st Corinthians 2:9 – That is what the Scriptures mean when they say, "No eye has seen, no ear has heard, and no mind has imagined what God has prepared for those who love Him."

Everybody in heaven is God's what? – Romans 8:16 – For His Spirit joins with our spirit to affirm that we are God's children.

Heaven belongs to those who are what? – Matthew 19:14 – But Jesus said, "Let the children come to me. Don't stop them! For the Kingdom of Heaven belongs to those who are like these children."

God's Face

Who will see God? – Matthew 5:8 – God blesses those whose hearts are pure, for they will see God.

Virtuous people will see whose face? – Psalm 11:7 – For the righteous Lord loves justice. The virtuous will see His face.

Will some people see the face of God? – Revelation 22:4 – And they will see His face, and His name will be written on their foreheads.

Job is going to see God with his what? – Job 19:27 – I will see Him for myself. Yes, I will see Him with my own eyes. I am overwhelmed at the thought!

Earthly and Eternal Bodies

God created every human being in His what? – Genesis 1:27 – So God created human beings in His own image. In the image of God He created them; male and female He created them.

Jesus is the visible image of the invisible who? – Colossians 1:15 – Christ is the visible image of the invisible God. He existed before anything was created and is supreme over all creation.

What are the two types of bodies? – 1st Corinthians 15:40 – There are also bodies in the heavens and bodies on the Earth. The glory of the heavenly bodies is different from the glory of the earthly bodies.

What comes first and what comes later? – 1st Corinthians 15:46 – What comes first is the natural body, then the spiritual body comes later.

Earthly people are like what kind of man? Heavenly people are like what kind of man? – 1ST Corinthians 15:48 – Earthly people are like the earthly man and heavenly people are like the heavenly man.

Someday, some people will be like what kind of man? – 1st Corinthians 15:49 – Just as we are now like the earthly man, we will someday be like the heavenly man.

Mortal bodies will be changed into what kind of bodies? – 1st Corinthians 15:53 – For our dying bodies must be transformed into bodies that will never die; our mortal bodies must be transformed into immortal bodies.

Will eternal bodies ever die? – 1st Corinthians 15:54 – Then, when our dying bodies have been transformed into bodies that will never die, this Scripture will be fulfilled: "Death is swallowed up in victory.

Eternal bodies made by God and not by human hands are found where? – 2nd Corinthians 5:1 – For we know that when this earthly tent we live in is taken down (that is, when we die and leave this earthly body), we will have a house in heaven, an eternal body made for us by God Himself and not by human hands.

People will have heavenly what? – 2nd Corinthians 5:3 – For we will put on heavenly bodies; we will not be spirits without bodies.

Earthly bodies will change into what kind of bodies? – Philippians 3:21 – He will take our weak mortal bodies and change them into glorious bodies like His own, using the same power with which He will bring everything under His control.

Paradise

What did Jesus tell the criminal that was on a cross next to Him? – Luke 23:43 – And Jesus replied, "I assure you, today you will be with me in paradise."

Caught up where? – 2nd Corinthians 12:4 – that I was caught up to paradise and heard things so astounding that they cannot be expressed in words, things no human is allowed to tell.

Tree of life is found where? – Revelation 2:7 – Anyone with ears to hear must listen to the Spirit and understand what He is saying to the churches. To everyone who is victorious I will give fruit from the tree of life in the paradise of God.

Permanently Disappear

Who is going to wipe away every tear? – Revelation 7:17 – For the Lamb on the throne will be their Shepherd. He will lead them to springs of life-giving water. And God will wipe every tear from their eyes."

What will be gone forever? – Revelation 21:4 – He will wipe every tear from their eyes and there will be no more death or sorrow or crying or pain. All these things are gone forever.

There will no longer be what upon anything? – Revelation 22:3 – No longer will there be a curse upon anything. For the throne of God and of the Lamb will be there and His servants will worship Him.

Decision Maker

How does God remain? – Psalm 102:27 – But you are always the same; you will live forever.

There is no what found in God? – 1st John 1:5 – This is the message we heard from Jesus and now declare to you: God is light and there is no darkness in Him at all.

God cannot tolerate what? – Psalm 5:4 – O God, you take no pleasure in wickedness; you cannot tolerate the sins of the wicked.

God cannot stand the sight of what? – Habakkuk 1:13 – But you are pure and cannot stand the sight of evil. Will you wink at their treachery? Should you be silent while the wicked swallow up people more righteous than they?

God wants everyone to keep their feet from what? – Proverbs 4:27 – Don't get sidetracked; keep your feet from following evil.

Everyone can be free from what? – Romans 6:18 – Now you are free from your slavery to sin, and you have become slaves to righteous living.

Everybody is a slave to whatever does what? – 2nd Peter 2:19 – They promise freedom, but they themselves are slaves of sin and corruption. For you are a slave to whatever controls you.

Work

What day did God rest? – Genesis 2:2 – On the seventh day God had finished His work of creation, so He rested from all His work.

God is always what? – John 5:17 – But Jesus replied, "My Father is always working, and so am I."

Adam worked in the what? – Genesis 2:15 – The LORD God placed the man in the Garden of Eden to tend and watch over it.

Do all of your work for the what of God? – 1st Corinthians 10:31 – So whether you eat or drink, or whatever you do, do it all for the glory of God.

Laughter

There is a time to do what? – Ecclesiastes 3:4 – A time to cry and a time to laugh. A time to grieve and a time to dance.

Personal Treasures

Why store up treasures in heaven? – Matthew 6:19-20 –Don't store up treasures here on Earth, where moths eat them and rust destroys them and where thieves break in and steal. Store your treasures in heaven, where moths and rust cannot destroy and thieves do not break in and steal.

Treasures will be what? – Luke 12:33 – Sell your possessions and give to those in need. This will store up treasure for you in heaven! And the purses of heaven never get old or develop holes. Your treasure will be safe; no thief can steal it and no moth can destroy it.

God and Humanity

Who is absolutely perfect? – Matthew 5:48 - But you are to be perfect, even as your Father in heaven is perfect.

Who is truly good? – Mark 10:18 – "Why do you call me good?" Jesus asked. "Only God is truly good.

God never does what? – James 1:17 – Whatever is good and perfect comes down to us from God our Father, who created all the lights in the heavens. He never changes or casts a shifting shadow.

Favoritism

Does God show any type of favoritism? – Job 34:19 – He doesn't care how great a person may be, and He pays no more attention to the rich than to the poor. He made them all.

God does not show what? – Romans 2:11 – For God does not show favoritism.

Humanity

God knows what about me? – Psalm 139:1 – O LORD, you have examined my heart and know everything about me.

How does God summon everyone? – Isaiah 45:3 – And I will give you treasures hidden in the darkness—secret riches. I will do this so you may know that I am the LORD, the God of Israel, the one who calls you by name.

What has God done with the palms of His hands? – Isaiah 49:16 – See, I have written your name on the palms of my hands. Always in my mind is a picture of Jerusalem's walls in ruins.

Faults of All Humanity

There is no one who does what? – Psalm 53:3 – But no, all have turned away; all have become corrupt. No one does good, not a single one!

No one is what? – Romans 3:10 – As the Scriptures say, "No one is righteous—not even one.

What does it say about everyone? – Romans 3:11 – No one is truly wise; no one is seeking God.

Cares and Thinks

God cares about what things? – Psalm 36:6 – Your righteousness is like the mighty mountains, your justice like the ocean depths. You care for people and animals alike, O LORD.

The same God does what? – Philippians 4:19 – And this same God who takes care of me will supply all your needs from His glorious riches, which have been given to us in Christ Jesus.

What are people to God? – Job 7:17 – What are people, that you should make so much of us, that you should think of us so often?

Does God think about people? – Psalm 139:17-18 – How precious are your thoughts about me, O God. They cannot be numbered! I can't even count them; they outnumber the grains of sand and when I wake up, you are still with me!

God does what things? – Psalm 8:4 – what are mere mortals that you should think about them, human beings that you should care for them?

Ears and Eyes

God made what things? – Proverbs 20:12 – Ears to hear and eyes to see—both are gifts from the LORD.

God is not what? – Psalm 94:9 – Is he deaf – the one who made your ears? Is he blind—the one who formed your eyes?

The ears of God are not? – Isaiah 59:1 – Listen! The LORD's arm is not too weak to save you, nor is His ear too deaf to hear you call.

God's ears are what? – Psalm 34:15 – The eyes of the LORD watch over those who do right; His ears are open to their cries for help.

Sees

God sees the whole what? – Psalm 33:13 – The LORD looks down from heaven and sees the whole human race.

Watches and Looks

God observes what? – Psalm 33:14 – From His throne He observes all who live on the Earth.

God watches what and sees what? – Job 34:21 – For God watches how people live; He sees everything they do.

God watches over you as you do what? – Psalm 121:8 – The LORD keeps watch over you as you come and go, both now and forever.

How does God watch everyone? – Psalm 11:4 – But the LORD is in His holy Temple; the LORD still rules from heaven. He watches everyone closely, examining every person on Earth.

God does what two things? – Proverbs 5:21 – For the LORD sees clearly what a man does, examining every path he takes.

Why does God look at the entire human race? – Psalm 14:2 – The LORD looks down from heaven on the entire human race; He looks to see if anyone is truly wise, if anyone seeks God.

What God Does

God does what? – Psalm 56:8 – You keep track of all my sorrows. You have collected all my tears in your bottle. You have recorded each one in your book.

The very what are numbered? – Matthew 10:30 – and the very hairs on your head are all numbered.

What is all numbered? Do not be what? – Luke 12:7 – And the very hairs on your head are all numbered. So don't be afraid; you are more valuable to God than a whole flock of sparrows.

How many steps of everyone does God number? – Job 31:4 – Doesn't He see everything I do and every step I take?

God knows when everyone does what? – Psalm 139:2 – You know when I sit down or stand up. You know my thoughts even when I'm far away.

What does God know about you? – Isaiah 37:28 – But I know you well—where you stay and when you come and go. I know the way you have raged against me.

What does God see? What does God know? – Psalms 139:3 – You see me when I travel and when I rest at home. You know everything I do.

What does God know about everybody? – Psalm 139:4 – You know what I am going to say even before I say it, LORD.

Predicting the Future

God is the only one who can do what? – Isaiah 46:10 – Only I can tell you the future before it even happens. Everything I plan will come to pass, for I do whatever I wish.

Does anybody know and are they able to predict the future? – Ecclesiastes 10:14 – they chatter on and on. No one really knows what is going to happen; no one can predict the future.

Enormity

Heaven is God's what? Earth is God's what? – Acts 7:49 – 'Heaven is my throne, and the Earth is my footstool. Could you build me a temple as good as that?' asks the LORD. 'Could you build me such a resting place?

God's what filled the temple? – Isaiah 6:1 – It was in the year King Uzziah died that I saw the Lord. He was sitting on a lofty throne, and the train of His robe filled the Temple.

God assigned the sea what? God locked the oceans in vast what? – Psalm 33:7 – He assigned the sea its boundaries and locked the oceans in vast reservoirs.

What has God done? – Isaiah 40:12 – Who else has held the oceans in His hand? Who has measured off the heavens with His fingers? Who else knows the weight of the Earth or has weighed the mountains and hills on a scale?

God does what? – Proverbs 30:4 – Who but God goes up to heaven and comes back down? Who holds the wind in His fists? Who wraps up the oceans in His cloak? Who has created the whole wide world? What is His name—and His son's name? Tell me if you know!

God picks up the whole earth as though it were what? – Isaiah 40:15 – No, for all the nations of the world are but a drop in the bucket. They are nothing more than dust on the scales. He picks up the whole Earth as though it were a grain of sand.

What is in His hand? – Psalm 95:4 – He holds in His hands the depths of the Earth and the mightiest mountains.

Children and Animals

What type of child will lead all of the animals? – Isaiah 11:6 – In that day the wolf and the lamb will live together; the leopard will lie down with the baby goat. The calf and the yearling will be safe with the lion and a little child will lead them all.

Who will play safely near the cobra snake hole? What type of child will put their hands into a nest of deadly snakes? – Isaiah 11:8 – The baby will play safely near the hole of a cobra. Yes, a little child will put its hand in a nest of deadly snakes without harm.

Will the animals get along? – Isaiah 11:7 – The cow will graze near the bear. The cub and the calf will lie down together. The lion will eat hay like a cow.

Who cares for the animals on the Earth? – Proverbs 12:10 – The godly care for their animals, but the wicked are always cruel.

Reunions

David begged who to spare his child? – 2ND Samuel 12:16 – David begged God to spare the child. He went without food and lay all night on the bare ground.

What happened to David and Bathsheba's child? – 2nd Samuel 12:18 – Then on the seventh day the child died. David's advisers were afraid to tell him. "He wouldn't listen to reason while the child was ill," they said. "What drastic thing will he do when we tell him the child is dead?"

David was told his child was what? – 2nd Samuel 12:19 – When David saw them whispering, he realized what had happened. "Is the child dead?" he asked. "Yes," they replied, "he is dead."

After David accepted his child's death, what did he do? – 2nd Samuel 12:20 – Then David got up from the ground, washed himself, put on lotions and changed his clothes. He went to the Tabernacle and worshiped the LORD. After that, he returned to the palace and was served food and ate.

His advisers were what regarding David's behavior? – 2ND Samuel 12:21 – His advisers were amazed. "We don't understand you," they told him. "While the child was still living, you wept and refused to eat. But now that the child is dead, you have stopped your mourning and are eating again."

Will David be reunited with his child? – 2ND Samuel 12:23 – But why should I fast when he is dead? Can I bring him back again? I will go to him one day, but he cannot return to me."

Tree of Life

The tree of life will bear what? – Revelation 22:1-3 – Then the angel showed me a river with the water of life, clear as crystal, flowing from the throne of God and of the Lamb. It flowed down the center of the main street. On each side of the river grew a tree of life, bearing twelve crops of fruit, with a fresh crop each month. The leaves were used for medicine to heal the nations. No longer will there be a curse upon anything. For the throne of God and of the Lamb will be there, and His servants will worship Him.

Festivals

What will be found inside God's temple? – Psalm 65:4 – What joy for those you choose to bring near, those who live in your holy courts. What festivities await us inside your holy Temple.

Future banquet and feast are described how? – Isaiah 25:6 – In Jerusalem, the LORD of Heaven's Armies will spread a wonderful feast for all the people of the world. It will be a delicious banquet with clear, well-aged wine and choice meat.

People will come from where? – Luke 13:29 – And people will come from all over the world—from east and west, north and south—to take their places in the Kingdom of God.

Blessed is the one who will what? – Luke 14:15 – Hearing this, a man sitting at the table with Jesus exclaimed, "What a blessing it will be to attend a banquet in the Kingdom of God!"

Laws

Who is the lawgiver? – Isaiah 33:22 – For the LORD is our judge, our lawgiver and our king. He will care for us and save us.

The laws of God are what? – Psalm 19:9 – Reverence for the LORD is pure, lasting forever. The laws of the LORD are true; each one is fair.

People should obey God's what? – Psalm 119:2 – Joyful are those who obey His laws and search for Him with all their hearts.

What are wonderful? – Psalm 119:129 – Your laws are wonderful. No wonder I obey them!

God's laws are what? – Psalm 119:138 – Your laws are perfect and completely trustworthy.

Safety and Protection

God will keep people what forever? – Psalm 37:28 – For the LORD loves justice and He will never abandon the godly. He will keep them safe forever, but the children of the wicked will die.

Who protects the oppressed forever? – Psalm 12:7 – Therefore, Lord, we know you will protect the oppressed, preserving them forever from this lying generation.

Peace and Unity

Who enforces peace in the heavens? – Job 25:2 – God is powerful and dreadful. He enforces peace in the heavens.

Godly will rest in what when they die? – Isaiah 57:2 – For those who follow godly paths will rest in peace when they die.

How does God bless His people? – Psalm 29:11 – The LORD gives His people strength. The LORD blesses them with peace.

God is not a God of disorder but of what? – 1st Corinthians 14:33 – For God is not a God of disorder but of peace, as in all the meetings of God's holy people.

God will keep people in perfect what? – Isaiah 26:3 – You will keep in perfect peace all who trust in you, all whose thoughts are fixed on you!

People of peace will have a what? – Psalm 37:37 – Look at those who are honest and good, for a wonderful future awaits those who love peace.

The peace I give is a what? Do not be what? – John 14:27 – I am leaving you with a gift—peace of mind and heart. And the peace I give is a gift the world cannot give. So don't be troubled or afraid.

Search for what? – 1st Peter 3:11 – Turn away from evil and do good. Search for peace, and work to maintain it.

Live in what with people? – Romans 12:16 – Live in harmony with each other. Don't be too proud to enjoy the company of ordinary people. And don't think you know it all!

Live at peace with? – Romans 12:18 – Do all that you can to live in peace with everyone.

How is living in harmony with people described? – Psalm 133:1 – How wonderful and pleasant it is when brothers live together in harmony!

Financial Status

Wealth does not follow anyone into what? – Psalm 49:17 – For when they die, they take nothing with them. Their wealth will not follow them into the grave.

Can anyone take their riches with them once they die? – Ecclesiastes 5:15 – We all come to the end of our lives as naked and empty-handed as on the day we were born. We can't take our riches with us.

What is very hard? – Matthew 19:23 – Then Jesus said to His disciples, "I tell you the truth, it is very hard for a rich person to enter the Kingdom of Heaven.

It is easier for a camel to what? – Matthew 19:24 – I'll say it again—it is easier for a camel to go through the eye of a needle than for a rich person to enter the Kingdom of God!

New Heaven and Earth

God will create what new things? – Isaiah 65:17 – Look! I am creating new heavens and a new earth, and no one will even think about the old ones anymore.

What will disappear in the future? – Revelation 21:1 – Then I saw a new heaven and a new earth, for the old heaven and the old earth had disappeared. and the sea was also gone.

What will remain forever? – Isaiah 66:22 – As surely as my new heavens and earth will remain, so will you always be my people, with a name that will never disappear," says the LORD.

We are to look forward to what? – 2nd Peter 3:13 – But we are looking forward to the new heavens and new earth he has promised, a world filled with God's righteousness.

Future New Jerusalem City

God has prepared what for the people? – Hebrews 11:16 – But they were looking for a better place, a heavenly homeland. That is why God is not ashamed to be called their God, for he has prepared a city for them.

The holy city is called what? – Revelation 21:2 – And I saw the holy city, the new Jerusalem, coming down from God out of heaven like a bride beautifully dressed for her husband.

The holy city will descend out of where? – Revelation 21:10 – So he took me in the Spirit to a great, high mountain, and he showed me the holy city, Jerusalem, descending out of heaven from God.

How many gates? – Revelation 21:12-13 – The city wall was broad and high, with twelve gates guarded by twelve angels. and the names of the twelve tribes of Israel were written on the gates. There were three gates on each side—east, north, south and west.

How many foundation stones? – Revelation 21:14 – The wall of the city had twelve foundation stones and on them were written the names of the twelve apostles of the Lamb.

What did the angel do with the measuring stick? – Revelation 21:15 – The angel who talked to me held in his hand a gold measuring stick to measure the city, its gates, and its wall.

The length, width, and height were how many miles? – Revelation 21:16 – When he measured it, he found it was a square, as wide as it was long. In fact, its length and width and height were each 1,400 miles.

How thick are the walls? – Revelation 21:17 – Then he measured the walls and found them to be 216 feet thick (according to the human standard used by the angel).

The wall was made of what? – Revelation 21:18 – The wall was made of jasper, and the city was pure gold, as clear as glass.

Jasper is as clear as what? – Revelation 21:11 – It shone with the glory of God and sparkled like a precious stone—like jasper as clear as crystal.

What precious stones will be found? – Revelation 21:19-20 – The wall of the city was built on foundation stones inlaid with twelve precious stones: the first was jasper, the second sapphire, the third agate, the fourth emerald, the fifth onyx, the sixth carnelian, the seventh chrysolite, the eighth beryl, the ninth topaz, the tenth chrysoprase, the eleventh jacinth, the twelfth amethyst.

The main street was what? – Revelation 21:21 – The twelve gates were made of pearls—each gate from a single pearl! and the main street was pure gold, as clear as glass.

Will the sun or moon exist? – Revelation 21:23 – And the city has no need of sun or moon, for the glory of God illuminates the city and the Lamb is its light.

Sun will never what? Moon will not do what? – Isaiah 60:20 – Your sun will never set; your moon will not go down. For the LORD will be your everlasting light. Your days of mourning will come to an end.

Will the gates ever be closed? – Revelation 21:25 – Its gates will never be closed at the end of day because there is no night there.

What will not be found? – Revelation 21:27 – Nothing evil will be allowed to enter, nor anyone who practices shameful idolatry and dishonesty—but only those whose names are written in the Lamb's Book of Life.

First row will contain what? – Exodus 28:17 – Mount four rows of gemstones on it. The first row will contain a red carnelian, a pale-green peridot, and an emerald.

Second row shall be what? – Exodus 28:18 – the second row shall be turquoise, lapis lazuli and emerald;

Third row will contain what? – Exodus 28:19 – The third row will contain an orange jacinth, an agate, and a purple amethyst.

Fourth row will contain what? – Exodus 28:20 – The fourth row will contain a blue-green beryl, an onyx, and a green jasper. All these stones will be set in gold filigree.

As God has said what? – 2nd Corinthians 6:16 – And what union can there be between God's temple and idols? For we are the temple of the living God. As God said: "I will live in them and walk among them. I will be their God, and they will be my people.

Jesus Predicted his Death

What was clearly predicted? – Luke 24:26 – Wasn't it clearly predicted that the Messiah would have to suffer all these things before entering His glory?"

Jesus will be handed over to be what? – Matthew 26:2 – "As you know, Passover begins in two days, and the Son of Man will be handed over to be crucified."

Who will reject Jesus? Jesus will be what? – Luke 9:22 – "The Son of Man must suffer many terrible things," he said. "He will be rejected by the elders, the leading priests, and the teachers of religious law. He will be killed, but on the third day He will be raised from the dead."

They will sentence Jesus to what? – Matthew 20:18 – "Listen," he said, "we're going up to Jerusalem, where the Son of Man will be betrayed to the leading priests and the teachers of religious law. They will sentence Him to die.

Jesus and the Entire Human Race

What weighed Jesus down? – Isaiah 53:4 – Yet it was our weaknesses He carried; it was our sorrows that weighed Him down. And we thought His troubles were a punishment from God, a punishment for His own sins!

Jesus died on the cross for what kind of people? – Romans 5:6 – When we were utterly helpless, Christ came at just the right time and died for us sinners.

Jesus purchased what? – Colossians 1:13-14 – For He has rescued us from the kingdom of darkness and transferred us into the Kingdom of His dear Son, who purchased our freedom and forgave our sins.

Jesus is the good shepherd who willingly sacrificed His life for what? – John 10:11 - I am the good shepherd. The good shepherd sacrifices His life for the sheep.

Jesus died for all of the sins of the entire what? – 1st John 2:2 – He Himself is the sacrifice that atones for our sins—and not only our sins but the sins of all the world.

Did Jesus ever sin? Was Jesus ever deceptive? – 1st Peter 2:22 – He never sinned, nor ever deceived anyone.

Jesus bore all of the sins of humanity in His what? – 1st Peter 2:24 – He personally carried our sins in His body on the cross so that we can be dead to sin and live for what is right. By His wounds you are healed.

Return of Jesus Back to the Earth

Who is the only person that knows the day and hour that Jesus will return back to the Earth? – Matthew 24:36 – "However, no one knows the day or hour when these things will happen, not even the angels in heaven or the Son Himself. Only the Father knows.

As it was in the days of Noah, the people were doing what? – Matthew 24:37-38 – "When the Son of Man returns, it will be like it was in Noah's day. In those days before the flood, the people were enjoying banquets and parties and weddings right up to the time Noah entered his boat.

People did not realize what? – Matthew 24:39 – People didn't realize what was going to happen until the flood came and swept them all away. That is the way it will be when the Son of Man comes.

Will the return of Jesus be visible to the entire human race? – Matthew 24:27 – For as the lightning flashes in the east and shines to the west, so it will be when the Son of Man comes.

Everyone needs to be what? – Mark 13:33 – And since you don't know when that time will come, be on guard! Stay alert!

Why should everyone keep watch? – Mark 13:35 – You, too, must keep watch! For you don't know when the master of the household will return—in the evening, at midnight, before dawn, or at daybreak.

When will Jesus return back to the Earth? – Luke 12:40 – You also must be ready all the time, for the Son of Man will come when least expected.

Day of the Lord

There will be greater what? It will never be what? – Matthew 24:21-22 – For there will be greater anguish than at any time since the world began. And it will never be so great again. In fact, unless that time of calamity is shortened, not a single person will survive. But it will be shortened for the sake of God's chosen ones.

Unless the Lord shortens that time of calamity, not a what? – Mark 13:19-20 – For there will be greater anguish in those days than at any time since God created the world. And it will never be so great again. In fact, unless the Lord shortens that time of calamity, not a single person will survive. But for the sake of His chosen ones he has shortened those days.

Scream in what? – Isaiah 13:6 – Scream in terror, for the day of the LORD has arrived—the time for the Almighty to destroy.

Arms are what in fear? Every heart will what? – Isaiah 13:7 – Every arm is paralyzed with fear. Every heart melts.

People are what? Pangs of what will grip them? Their faces will be what with fear? – Isaiah 13:8 – and people are terrified. Pangs of anguish grip them, like those of a woman in labor. They look helplessly at one another, their faces aflame with fear.

How is the day described? – Isaiah 13:9 – For see, the day of the LORD is coming—the terrible day of His fury and fierce anger. The land will be made desolate, and all the sinners destroyed with it.

Stars will give no what? Sun will be what? Moon will provide no what? – Isaiah 13:10 – The heavens will be black above them; the stars will give no light. The sun will be dark when it rises, and the moon will provide no light.

Why will God punish the entire world? – Isaiah 13:11 – I, the LORD, will punish the world for its evil and the wicked for their sin. I will crush the arrogance of the proud and humble the pride of the mighty.

What will be shaken? The Earth will move from its what? How is His anger described? – Isaiah 13:13 – For I will shake the heavens. The Earth will move from its place when the LORD of Heaven's Armies displays His wrath in the day of His fierce anger.

Sinning

A person who keeps all of the laws except one law is what? – James 2:10 – For the person who keeps all of the laws except one is as guilty as a person who has broken all of God's laws.

Not a single person is always what? – Ecclesiastes 7:20 – Not a single person on Earth is always good and never sins.

How many people have sinned? – Romans 3:23 – For everyone has sinned; we all fall short of God's glorious standard.

People who are leading a rebellious life will suffer for their what? – Psalm 107:17 – Some were fools; they rebelled and suffered for their sins.

When people claim to be sinless, what are they doing? – 1st John 1:8 – If we claim we have no sin, we are only fooling ourselves and not living in the truth.

Sinless

Was Jesus guilty of any type of sins? – John 8:46 – Which of you can truthfully accuse me of sin? And since I am telling you the truth, why don't you believe me?

Jesus never did what? – 2nd Corinthians 5:21 – For God made Christ, who never sinned, to be the offering for our sin, so that we could be made right with God through Christ.

Sins

What kind of sins are seen by God? – Psalm 90:8 – You spread out our sins before you—our secret sins—and you see them all.

Sins will find you what? – Numbers 32:23 – But if you fail to keep your word, then you will have sinned against the LORD, and you may be sure that your sin will find you out.

When people know to do good, but they opt not to do good, it is what? – James 4:17 – Remember, it is sin to know what you ought to do and then not do it.

Strive to Change the Wrongs in Life

Do not be enslaved by what? – 1st Corinthians 7:23 – God paid a high price for you, so don't be enslaved by the world.

Everyone should do what? Run away from what? – Amos 5:14-15 – Do what is good and run from evil so that you may live!

Then the LORD God of Heaven's Armies will be your helper, just as you have claimed.

What does God detest? – Proverbs 12:22 – The LORD detests lying lips, but He delights in those who tell the truth.

Stop doing what? – Hosea 4:2 – You make vows and break them; you kill and steal and commit adultery. There is violence everywhere—one murder after another.

Get rid of what things? – James 1:21 – So get rid of all the filth and evil in your lives and humbly accept the word God has planted in your hearts, for it has the power to save your souls.

How are the lives of people described? – Romans 1:29 – Their lives became full of every kind of wickedness, sin, greed, hate, envy, murder, quarreling, deception, malicious behavior and gossip.

Do not be what? – Romans 1:30 – They are backstabbers, haters of God, insolent, proud and boastful. They invent new ways of sinning and they disobey their parents.

Put to death what things? – Colossians 3:5 – So put to death the sinful, earthly things lurking within you. Have nothing to do with sexual immorality, impurity, lust and evil desires. Don't be greedy, for a greedy person is an idolater, worshiping the things of this world.

Get rid of what things? – Colossians 3:8 – But now is the time to get rid of anger, rage, malicious behavior, slander and dirty language.

Get rid of what? – 1st Peter 2:1 – So get rid of all evil behavior. Be done with all deceit, hypocrisy, jealousy and all unkind speech.

Turn from what and do good? – Psalm 34:14 – Turn away from evil and do good. Search for peace, and work to maintain it.

Ten Commandments

If you love me, do what? – John 14:15 – If you love me, obey my commandments.

You are my friends if you do what? – John 15:14 – You are my friends if you do what I command.

Do not do what? – Exodus 20:3 – You must not have any other god but me.

Do not do what? – Exodus 20:4-6 – You must not make for yourself an idol of any kind or an image of anything in the heavens or on the earth or in the sea. You must not bow down to them or worship them, for I, the LORD your God, am a jealous God who will not tolerate your affection for any other gods. I lay the sins of the parents upon their children; the entire family is affected—even children in the third and fourth generations of those who reject me. But I lavish unfailing love for a thousand generations on those who love me and obey my commands.

Do not do what? – Exodus 20:7 – You must not misuse the name of the LORD your God. The LORD will not let you go unpunished if you misuse His name.

Keep what holy? – Exodus 20:8-11 – Remember the Sabbath day by keeping it holy. Six days you shall labor and do all your work, but the seventh day is a sabbath to the LORD your God. On it you shall not do any work, neither you, nor your son or daughter, nor your male or female servant, nor your animals, nor any foreigner residing in your towns. For in six days the LORD made the heavens and the earth, the sea, and all that is in them, but He rested on the seventh day. Therefore, the LORD blessed the Sabbath day and made it holy.

Honor whom? – Exodus 20:12 – Honor your father and mother. Then you will live a long, full life in the land the LORD your God is giving you.

Do not do what? – Exodus 20:13 – You must not murder.

Do not do what? – Exodus 20:14 – You must not commit adultery.

Do not do what? – Exodus 20:15 – You must not steal.

Do not do what? – Exodus 20:16 – You must not testify falsely against your neighbor.

Do not do what? – Exodus 20:17 - You must not covet your neighbor's house. You must not covet your neighbor's wife, male or female servant, ox or donkey, or anything else that belongs to your neighbor."

Jesus

Jesus came to do what? – Luke 19:10 – For the Son of Man came to seek and save those who are lost.

Jesus did what for all of our sins? – 1st Corinthians 15:3 – I passed on to you what was most important and what had also been passed on to me. Christ died for our sins, just as the Scriptures said.

Who is the mediator? – 1st Timothy 2:5 – For there is only one God and one Mediator who can reconcile God and humanity—the man Christ Jesus.

God is only accessible through who? – John 14:6 – Jesus told him, "I am the way, the truth, and the life. No one can come to the Father except through me.

Salvation (Born Again)

People must be what? – John 3:3 – Jesus replied, "I tell you the truth, unless you are born again, you cannot see the Kingdom of God."

People who accept Jesus will be what? – Romans 10:13 – For "Everyone who calls on the name of the LORD will be saved."

Who is the gate? – John 10:9 – Yes, I am the gate. Those who come in through me will be saved. They will come and go freely and will find good pastures.

Salvation comes from who? – Revelation 7:10 – And they were shouting with a great roar, "Salvation comes from our God who sits on the throne and from the Lamb!"

There is salvation in what? – Acts 4:12 – There is salvation in no one else! God has given no other name under heaven by which we must be saved.

People who believe shall be what? – Mark 16:16 – Anyone who believes and is baptized will be saved. But anyone who refuses to believe will be condemned.

How will you be saved? – Romans 10:9 – If you openly declare that Jesus is Lord and believe in your heart that God raised Him from the dead, you will be saved.

For people who acknowledge Jesus, He will do what? – Matthew 10:32 – Everyone who acknowledges me publicly here on Earth, I will also acknowledge before my Father in heaven.

Free gift of God is what? – Romans 6:23 – For the wages of sin is death, but the free gift of God is eternal life through Christ Jesus our Lord.

God saves people by His what? – Ephesians 2:8-9 – God saved you by His grace when you believed. and you can't take credit for this; it is a gift from God. Salvation is not a reward for the good things we have done, so none of us can boast about it.

How is eternal life obtained? – John 3:16 – For this is how God loved the world: He gave His one and only Son, so that everyone who believes in Him will not perish but have eternal life.

If you believe in Jesus, you will know what? – 1st John 5:13 – I have written this to you who believe in the name of the Son of God, so that you may know you have eternal life.

No one can do what? – John 10:28 – I give them eternal life, and they will never perish. No one can snatch them away from me.

Let all of the world do what? – Isaiah 45:22 – Let all the world look to me for salvation! For I am God; there is no other.

God wants everyone to be what? – 1st Timothy 2:3:4 – This is good and pleases God our Savior, who wants everyone to be saved and to understand the truth.

Rejection

Make sure that you never do what? – Hebrews 12:25 – Be careful that you do not refuse to listen to the One who is speaking. For if the people of Israel did not escape when they refused to listen to Moses, the earthly messenger, we will certainly not escape if we reject the One who speaks to us from heaven!

Soul

Do not forfeit your what? – Mark 8:36-37 – And what do you benefit if you gain the whole world but lose your own soul? Is anything worth more than your soul?

Seeking and Hardening

Seek out Jesus while you can do what? – Isaiah 55:6 – Seek the LORD while you can find Him. Call on Him now while He is near.

Do not harden your what? – Hebrews 4:7 – So God set another time for entering His rest, and that time is today. God announced this through David much later in the words already quoted: "Today when you hear His voice, don't harden your hearts."

Repent

God wants everybody to do what? – 2nd Peter 3:9 – The Lord isn't really being slow about His promise, as some people think. No, He is being patient for your sake. He does not want anyone to be destroyed, but wants everyone to repent.

God's kindness is intended to turn people from what? – Romans 2:4 – Don't you see how wonderfully kind, tolerant, and patient God is with you? Does this mean nothing to you? Can't you see that His kindness is intended to turn you from your sin?

Do what things regarding the Good News? – Mark 1:14-15 – Later on, after John was arrested, Jesus went into Galilee, where he preached God's Good News. "The time promised by God has come at last!" he announced. "The Kingdom of God is near! Repent of your sins and believe the Good News!"

Confesssed Sins

God is ready to do what? – Psalm 86:5 – O Lord, you are so good, so ready to forgive, so full of unfailing love for all who ask for your help.

When people confess and ask for the forgiveness of their sins, God will remove them as far as the what? – Psalm 103:12 – He has removed our sins as far from us as the east is from the west.

When people confess and ask forgiveness of all of their sins, God will throw our sins where? – Micah 7:19 – Once again you will have compassion on us. You will trample our sins under your feet and throw them into the depths of the ocean!

What does God do regarding our confessed sins and offenses? – Isaiah 44:22 – I have swept away your sins like a cloud. I have scattered your offenses like the morning mist. Oh, return to me, for I have paid the price to set you free."

God will make sins white as what when He forgives all of them? – Isaiah 1:18 – "Come now, let's settle this," says the LORD. "Though your sins are like scarlet, I will make them as white as snow. Though they are red like crimson, I will make them as white as wool.

God will cleanse and forgive all their what? – Jeremiah 33:8 – I will cleanse them of their sins against me and forgive all their sins of rebellion.

God does what regarding our sins? – Isaiah 43:25 – "I—yes, I alone—will blot out your sins for my own sake and will never think of them again.

What can be wiped away if they are repented? – Acts 3:19 – Now repent of your sins and turn to God, so that your sins may be wiped away.

Lazarus

How is the rich man described? – Luke 16:19 – Jesus said, "There was a certain rich man who was splendidly clothed in purple and fine linen and who lived each day in luxury.

Lazarus was what? – Luke 16:20 – At his gate lay a poor man named Lazarus who was covered with sores.

Lazarus wanted what off of the rich man's table? – Luke 16:21 – As Lazarus lay there longing for scraps from the rich man's table, the dogs would come and lick his open sores.

Rich man is in what because of the flames in hell? – Luke 16:24 – 'The rich man shouted, 'Father Abraham, have some pity!

Send Lazarus over here to dip the tip of his finger in water and cool my tongue. I am in anguish in these flames.'

Rich man is what in hell? – Luke 16:25 - But Abraham said to him, 'Son, remember that during your lifetime you had everything you wanted, and Lazarus had nothing. So now he is here being comforted, and you are in anguish.

Rich man wants someone to do what, so his brothers do not join him? – Luke 16:28 – For I have five brothers and I want him to warn them so they don't end up in this place of torment.

Tower of Babel

All of the people spoke the same what and used the same what? – Genesis 11:1 – At one time all the people of the world spoke the same language and used the same words.

The people migrated to the what? – Genesis 11:2 – As the people migrated to the east, they found a plain in the land of Babylonia and settled there.

What did the people want to do for themselves? – Genesis 11:4 – Then they said, "Come, let's build a great city for ourselves with a tower that reaches into the sky. This will make us famous and keep us from being scattered all over the world."

God came down to do what? – Genesis 11:5 – But the LORD came down to look at the city and the tower the people were building.

God saw that the people are what? They spoke the same what? – Genesis 11:6 - "Look!" he said. "The people are united, and they all speak the same language. After this, nothing they set out to do will be impossible for them!

God said what? – Genesis 11:7 – Come, let's go down and confuse the people with different languages. Then they won't be able to understand each other.

God scattered all of the people where? – Genesis 11:8 – In that way, the LORD scattered them all over the world, and they stopped building the city.

What did God do? – Genesis 11:9 – That is why the city was called Babel, because that is where the LORD confused the people with different languages. In this way He scattered them all over the world.

Noah

What did God see? – Genesis 6:5 – The LORD observed the extent of human wickedness on the Earth, and He saw that everything they thought or imagined was consistently and totally evil.

What did God regret? – Genesis 6:6 – So the LORD was sorry He had ever made them and put them on the Earth. It broke His heart.

God said what? – Genesis 6:7 – And the LORD said, "I will wipe this human race I have created from the face of the Earth. Yes, and I will destroy every living thing—all the people, the large animals, the small animals that scurry along the ground, and even the birds of the sky. I am sorry I ever made them."

Noah found what in the eyes of God? – Genesis 6:8 – But Noah found favor with the LORD.

Noah was what kind of man? – Genesis 6:9 – This is the account of Noah and his family. Noah was a righteous man, the only blameless person living on Earth at the time and he walked in close fellowship with God.

Earth had become what? Earth was full of what? – Genesis 6:11 - Now God saw that the Earth had become corrupt and was filled with violence.

What did God say? – Genesis 6:13 – So God said to Noah, "I have decided to destroy all living creatures, for they have filled the Earth with violence. Yes, I will wipe them all out along with the Earth!

God told Noah to do what? – Genesis 6:14 – Build a large boat from cypress wood and waterproof it with tar, inside and out. Then construct decks and stalls throughout its interior.

Who was forewarned? – Hebrews 11:7 – It was by faith that Noah built a large boat to save his family from the flood. He obeyed God, who warned him about things that had never happened before. By his faith Noah condemned the rest of the world, and he received the righteousness that comes by faith.

How big was the ark built? – Genesis 6:15-16 – Make the boat 450 feet long, 75 feet wide and 45 feet high. Leave an 18-inch opening below the roof all the way around the boat. Put the door on the side and build three decks inside the boat—lower, middle and upper.

How did God wait while the ark was being built? – 1st Peter 3:20 – those who disobeyed God long ago when God waited patiently while Noah was building his boat. Only eight people were saved from drowning in that terrible flood.

Flood will destroy all of what? – Genesis 6:17 – Look! I am about to cover the Earth with a flood that will destroy every living thing that breathes. Everything on Earth will die.

People were doing what things? – Luke 17:27 – In those days, the people enjoyed banquets and parties and weddings right up to the time Noah entered his boat and the flood came and destroyed them all.

God told Noah what? – Genesis 6:18 – But I will confirm my covenant with you. So enter the boat—you and your wife and your sons and their wives.

Bring a pair of what? – Genesis 6:19-20 – Bring a pair of every kind of animal—a male and a female—into the boat with you to keep them alive during the flood. Pairs of every kind of bird, and every kind of animal, and every kind of small animal that scurries along the ground, will come to you to be kept alive.

Take with you how many pairs? – Genesis 7:2-3 – Take with you seven pairs—male and female—of each animal I have approved for eating and for sacrifice and take one pair of each of the others. Also take seven pairs of every kind of bird. There must be a male and a female in each pair to ensure that all life will survive on the Earth after the flood.

What kinds of animals? – Genesis 7:8-9 – With them were all the various kinds of animals—those approved for eating and for sacrifice and those that were not—along with all the birds and the small animals that scurry along the ground. They entered the boat in pairs, male and female, just as God had commanded Noah.

What kind of animals went into the ark? – Genesis 7:14-15 – With them in the boat were pairs of every kind of animal—domestic and wild, large and small—along with birds of every kind. Two by two they came into the boat, representing every living thing that breathes.

What was stored in the ark for Noah and his family, together for all of the animals? – Genesis 6:21 – And be sure to take on board enough food for your family and for all the animals.

Did Noah do exactly what God commanded? – Genesis 6:22 – So Noah did everything exactly as God had commanded him.

How many days was it going to rain on the Earth? – Genesis 7:4 – Seven days from now I will make the rains pour down on the Earth. And it will rain for forty days and forty nights, until I have wiped from the Earth all the living things I have created."

Why did Noah and his family go into the ark? – Genesis 7:6-7 – Noah was 600 years old when the flood covered the Earth. He went on board the boat to escape the flood—he and his wife and his sons and their wives.

Who closed the ark door? – Genesis 7:13-16 – That very day Noah had gone into the boat with his wife and his sons—Shem, Ham, Japheth—and their wives. With them in the boat were pairs of every kind of animal—domestic and wild, large and small—along with birds of every kind. Two by two they came into the boat, representing every living thing that breathes. A male and female of each kind entered, just as God had commanded Noah. Then the LORD closed the door behind them.

After seven days, the flood waters did what? – Genesis 7:10 – After seven days, the waters of the flood came and covered the Earth.

How did the rain fall? – Genesis 7:11 – When Noah was 600 years old, on the seventeenth day of the second month, all the underground waters erupted from the Earth and the rain fell in mighty torrents from the sky.

Ark was lifted high above the what? – Genesis 7:17-18 – For forty days the floodwaters grew deeper, covering the ground and lifting the boat high above the Earth. As the waters rose higher and higher above the ground, the boat floated safely on the surface.

Water covered what? – Genesis 7:19-20 – Finally, the water covered even the highest mountains on the Earth, rising more than twenty-two feet above the highest peaks.

What died? – Genesis 7:21-23 – All the living things on Earth died—birds, domestic animals, wild animals, small animals that scurry along the ground and all the people. Everything that breathed and lived on dry land died. God wiped out every living thing on the Earth—people, livestock, small animals that scurry along the ground and the birds of the sky. All were destroyed. The only people who survived were Noah and those with him in the boat.

What kind of people did God destroy with the vast flood? – 2nd Peter 2:5 – and God did not spare the ancient world—except for Noah and the seven others in his family. Noah warned the world of God's righteous judgment. So God protected Noah when He destroyed the world of ungodly people with a vast flood.

Waters flooded the Earth for how many days? – Genesis 7:24 – And the floodwaters covered the Earth for 150 days.

Who did God remember? – Genesis 8:1 – But God remembered Noah and all the wild animals and the livestock that were with him in the ark and He sent a wind over the Earth and the waters receded.

Every time there is a rainbow this is God's covenant that He makes with you and what? – Genesis 9:13 – I have placed my rainbow in the clouds. It is the sign of my covenant with you and with all the Earth.

A rainbow is what kind of covenant? – Genesis 9:16 – When I see the rainbow in the clouds, I will remember the eternal covenant between God and every living creature on Earth.

After the flood, Noah lived how long? – Genesis 9:28 – Noah lived another 350 years after the great flood.

EPILOGUE

We are all sinners. Nobody takes a day off from sin; instead, everyone in the human race becomes a slave to all kinds of evils. The Bible teaches us that the penalty of sin is death, an immutable sentence which must be paid in full. However, the reality is, nobody can make one payment towards their sin wages. It is an impossibility. How will all of the sin wages be paid?

There was only one person who never sinned. His name is Jesus. He was born, lived a perfect life for 33 years, and then died an abysmal and appalling death on the cross to atone for the entire human race. Jesus paid every sin wage for all of humanity in total. His death paid the penalty for every sin that ever was or will be committed. But we must have our death sentence pardoned before our physical death, before we cross over to our eternal destiny.

Every human being shares a common denominator. We are born, live on Earth, die, and immediately enter the afterlife.

The majority of people are scared of dying because of the unknown. There are two perspectives of death: mourning and celebrating. God does not hide any undisclosed facts; instead, He deliberately ensures that nobody is surprised upon their arrival into the unknown. The Bible clearly shows what happens before we are born into this life, and what happens when we die and enter the afterlife.

The afterlife does exist. Everybody is going to permanently reside in heaven or hell. One location is optimum, and the other location is atrocious. Choosing our afterlife residency, is a personal choice. Because God has given everyone free will, He will never interfere and try to change our chosen afterlife decisions. God will grant the preferences of everybody. One of the greatest gifts God has given us is the freedom to choose. Without choice, there are only mandates, and God desires an intimate and interactive relationship with each of us. It's why He created us in the first place.

There are good things and bad things found in the two locations of the afterlife. However, these destinations do not have a mixed bag. It will either be one or the other. Heaven has all good things. Hell has all bad things.

The world is guilty of judging people and putting them into categories of either good or bad for various reasons. The shocking eye-opener is that good and bad people, by human standards, are found in both heaven and hell. Your goodness or badness has nothing to do with where you will spend eternity, only your willingness to make Christ Lord over your life.

While living on Earth, everybody found in hell decided they did not want to submit to God. They made their personal choices to rebel and disobey God, refusing to repent and never confessing and asking for the forgiveness of their sins. As a result of their decisions, everyone found in hell is the enemy of God. They turned their backs on God. He is now turning His back on them. The Bible teaches in Hebrews 10:31, "It is a terrible thing to fall into the hands of the living God."

All people put their dependency on the wrong things. They counted on trying to be a good person, having high moral standards, doing good deeds, giving to worthy charities, listening to false spiritual leaders, and refusing to accept the absolute truth that God, Jesus, and the afterlife exists. Also, they believed there were other options available for them to choose from that would have stopped them from being sent to hell.

Everyone in heaven decided that they wanted to belong to God. No one in heaven is an enemy of God. This reality is

Epilogue

because everybody put their total dependency on Jesus dying for their sins on the cross to get them into heaven. Everyone accepted Jesus and made Him the Lord and Savior of their lives.

Once a person enters hell, it is too late for things to change for them. There are no do-overs. Nobody can clean up their life so they can be released from here and sent back to the Earth to relive their lives pleasing God. Also, no one is ever granted permission to be sent to heaven after a certain amount of time has elapsed. Hell is non-escapable and eternal; therefore, everybody is trapped and unable to escape.

Everyone in heaven does not want anything to change. Heaven is perfect in every way. Nobody has any plans to escape. On the contrary, they are happier now than they were while living on Earth. They are living in community the way God originally intended it to be.

Before entering the afterlife, every person needs to comparison shop the two options.

God is absent in hell. He created hell for Satan and the demons.

God is in heaven. God desires for all people to spend eternity with their creator in heaven.

Satan is the great deceiver. He is a liar who convinces people that the best location in the afterlife is hell. God is not a liar but tells the truth at all times. He teaches in the Bible for everyone to avoid hell at all costs and choose to live in heaven with Him for eternity.

God and the Bible go hand-in-hand. God inspired the entire Bible from Genesis to Revelation. He is forewarning and putting every person in the whole of the human race on red alert because of future events, and to proclaim His love for us so that we may be spared.

Do not procrastinate in making your personal afterlife decision. Think long and hard about where you want to permanently reside in the afterlife for trillions and trillions and trillions of years that will never come to an end.

If you opt to go to <u>hell</u> (appalling location), continue to live your life the way you are and make no changes to your current lifestyle. Refuse God's gift of salvation. Turn your back on Jesus and reject Him.

If you want to go to <u>heaven</u> (picture-perfect location) after you die, you need to do the following:

1. Embrace God's gift of salvation, ask forgiveness of all of your sins, and accept Jesus as your Lord and Savior.
2. Pray this simple prayer – Lord Jesus, I am a sinner. I repent of my sins. I make you my <u>Lord and Savior</u>. Amen.
3. <u>Great news</u>. If you do the things mentioned above, you will belong to God, become His child, and live with Him forever and ever.
4. The <u>Best News</u> is that you can never lose your salvation because nobody can snatch you away from God.

I genuinely hope to meet you in heaven one day.

ABOUT THE AUTHOR

Vi Lindemuth is a child of God because she belongs to Him. When she was a young teen, she asked Jesus to forgive her sins and made Him the Lord and Savior of her life. During the years after, Vi continued to grow in ministry and fellowship with fellow believers. In addition, her work in the legal field for years, both as a court reporter and in a law office, honed her eye for ascertaining facts and discerning truth. A native of Pennsylvania, Vi spent over twenty years in northern Virginia before returning home.

She has two missions in her life to fulfill. One of her missions is to make the truth known about the afterlife. Her other goal in life is to remind heaven-bound people that their life on earth is temporary. Their impeccable future residency in Heaven will be permanent and never-ending for trillions of years with no ending in sight. When Vi thinks of her permanent residency, it always puts a smile on her face.

www.ingramcontent.com/pod-product-compliance
Lightning Source LLC
Chambersburg PA
CBHW062206080426
42734CB00010B/1816